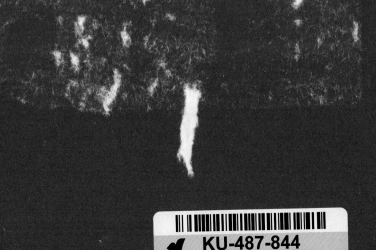

THIMBLES

The thimble-maker. *After an engraving by Jost Amman (1539-1591)*

THIMBLES

Edwin F. Holmes

Gill and Macmillan

First published in 1976

Gill and Macmillan Ltd
15/17 Eden Quay
Dublin 1
and internationally through
association with the
Macmillan Publishers Group

7171 0762 0

Jacket and text designed by Dermot McGuinne
Colour by Criterion Press, Dublin
Typesetting by Les Presses Saint-Augustin, Bruges

Printed in Great Britain by
Fletcher & Son Ltd, Norwich

Tine [lose] thimble,
    tine thrift.

Old Scottish proverb

Acknowledgements

It would not be possible for me to mention individually all the persons and all the organisations who have either volunteered information or else patiently answered my queries but among many others my thanks are due to the following: David Addison B.A., Dip. Ed., A.M.A. of the Cheltenham Art Gallery and Museum; Mrs Elizabeth Aldridge; D.M. Bailey of the Department of Greek and Roman Antiquities of the British Museum; Rosemary A. Bower of the Derby Museums and Art Gallery; The Reading Room Information Service of the British Library; Mrs K. Butler of the State Hermitage Museum, Leningrad; Sig. Raffaello Causa of the Neapolitan Museums service; R. J. Charleston of the Victoria and Albert Museum, and the staff of the Victoria and Albert Museum Library; John Clark of the City of London Guildhall Museum; Mrs S. Davis; The Royal Doulton Group; Dr I. H. van Eeghen of the Gemeentelijke Archiefdienst van Amsterdam; Conservateur H. P. Fourest of the Musée National de Céramique, Sèvres; L. S. Garrad of the Manx Museum; Dr Tjark Hausmann of the Kunstgewerbemuseum, Berlin; Frau Ursula Hildt; F. C. Hunt Esq.; The Central Library of the Borough of Islington; Dr Hermann Jedding of the Museum für Kunst und Gewerbe, Hamburg; The Kendal Library, Cumberland; Dr Ekkart Klinge of the Landeshaupstadt, Düsseldorf; Mrs C. Kuttschrütter; Mildred B. Lanier of the Colonial Williamsburg Foundation; Director Erik Lassen of the Museum of Decorative Art, Copenhagen; Miss Cynthia Leavens; The Marlow Library, Buckinghamshire; The VEB Staatliche Porzellan-Manufaktur, Meissen; The Metropolitan Museum of Art, New York; A. R. Mountford, M.A., F.M.A., F.S.A., of the City of Stoke-on-Trent Museum and Art Gallery; Miss A. M. Louise E. Mulder-Erkelens of the Rijksmuseum, Amsterdam; A. A. van der Poel of the Zeeuws Museum, Middelburg; Mlle Olga Popovitch, Conservateur des Musées de Rouen; Dr Anna Rapp of the Schweizerisches Landesmuseum, Zurich; J. F. Russell, M. A. of the Department of Medieval and Later Antiquities of the British Museum; Professor A. Salonen; Mr Henry Sandon of the Worcester Royal Porcelain Co. Ltd.; Dr Günter Schade of the DDR Staatliche Museum zu Berlin; Baron Jean Seillière; Mme G. Sennequier of the Musée des Antiquités, Rouen; Mrs A. D. Silvester; Mrs Joan Sinclair; Miss Kay Staniland of the London Museum; Mr and Mrs L. Stewart; Dr H. Waetzoldt; John W. Waterer, R.D.I., F.S.A., F.S.I.A., of the Museum of Leathercraft; Mr and Mrs Graham Webb. To all these and to many besides I offer my grateful thanks.

The colour illustrations are reproduced largely from private sources and I am grateful to those concerned. Plate 3 *(above)* is reproduced by courtesy of the Museum für Kunst und Gewerbe, Hamburg; Plate 3 *(below)* by courtesy of the Trustees of the Victoria and Albert Museum; Plate 8 *(above)* by courtesy of the Trustees of the British Museum. Mr Michael Holford was responsible for much of the photography, namely Plates 2, 3 *(below)*, 5 *(above right)*, 6, 7, 8 *(below left and right)*.

For permission to reproduce the black-and-white photographs of specimens or pictures from their collection, my grateful thanks are tendered to the following: fig. 1, Musée des Antiquités, Rouen; fig. 3, The Metropolitan Museum of Art, New York (Rogers Fund, 1910); fig. 4, Zeeuws Museum, Middelburg; fig. 5, The Trustees of the City of London Guildhall Museum; fig. 6, The Trustees of the London Museum; fig. 8, The Trustees of the National Gallery, London; fig. 9, Fries Museum, Leeuwarden; fig. 15, The Trustees of the British Museum; fig. 17, The Colonial Williamsburg Foundation; fig. 27, Yale University Art Gallery (The Mabel Brady Garvan Collection); fig. 28, Museum of Fine Arts, Boston (Gift of Mrs Henry B. Chapin and Edward H. R. Revere); fig. 38, Gebrüder Gabler G.m.b.H.; fig. 39, Messrs Henry Griffith and Sons Limited; fig. 40, Central Museum, Utrecht; fig. 43, The Colonial Williamsburg Foundation; fig. 44, Schweiz. Landesmuseum, Zurich; fig. 73, Musée Le Secq des Tournelles, Rouen; fig. 115, Stedelijk Museum, Amsterdam; fig. 116, Staatliche Kunsthalle, Karlsruhe. The remaining black-and-white illustrations are reproduced from private sources and in this connection I am indebted to Mr Angelo Hornak, to Mr W. A. Skarrat of Wallace Heaton Limited and to Mr C. K. Shah.

Finally with regard to the production of this book, I would like to thank Mr Bill Smith who suggested it, Mr Gerald Pollinger who made it possible and my publishers Messrs Gill and Macmillan Limited and more particularly Miss Mary Dowey and Miss Bridget Lunn for their help and guidance.

Contents

Introduction 1

Early thimbles 6

Eighteenth-century thimbles 18

Porcelain thimbles 30

Enamel thimbles 38

Gold thimbles 44

Mother-of-pearl thimbles 48

Ivory thimbles 53

Tortoise-shell thimbles 56

Silver thimbles 57

Bone thimbles 80

Horn thimbles 81

Leather thimbles 82

Glass thimbles 83

Stone thimbles 84

Wooden thimbles 87

Fabric thimbles 89

Brass thimbles 90

Other base metal thimbles 97

Plastic thimbles 105

Tailors' thimbles 106

Children's thimbles 108

Souvenir thimbles 109

Advertising thimbles 115

Finger guards 118

Just a thimbleful 120

Thimble cases 122

Thimble-rigging 135

Collecting thimbles 141

Bibliography 146

Notes 147

Index 149

Introduction

The idea of protecting the finger when sewing with a needle is presumably as old as the invention of the needle itself and goes back into antiquity. It is unlikely however that we shall ever be able to retrace the steps which brought the thimble into existence. For one thing archeologists studying the ancient civilisations seldom come across thimbles. The noted egyptologist, Sir William M. Flinders Petrie, records only one thimble in his *Tools and Weapons* (London 1917) – a bronze ring-type thimble of probable late Roman origin – which suggests that although there is ample evidence that the needle was commonplace in ancient Egypt, the thimble as we know it was unknown. Similarly, G. R. Davidson writing on the subject of the excavations at Corinth states that there is no evidence that the thimble was used in Corinth before the Byzantine period and he adds that 'thimbles do not seem to have existed anywhere before Roman times'.[1] Nevertheless it is difficult to believe that the Romans were the first to use thimbles. One possibility to account for the lack of remains is that early thimbles were made of leather, a material which is prone to decay, but this cannot be confirmed. Early pictures and drawings are of little help. The Egyptian tomb paintings, for instance, represent many activities in considerable detail but nowhere does the thimble appear. And neither is there any help to be found in the written word. Thimbles may conceivably be mentioned in cuneiform, hieroglyphic or other writings but if so the meaning has been lost and no such references have been deciphered. There is therefore a total and impenetrable lack of information regarding the early history of the thimble and at best its development remains a matter of conjecture.

It is tempting to speculate that the earliest tool resembling a thimble was a piece of stone or bone held in the hand and used to push through a needle. There is some support for this theory in the discovery of a small stone implement at El Lisht in the Nile Valley which is now in the safe-keeping of the Metropolitan Museum of Art in New York. This is reputed to be a needle pusher dating from the XXth-XXIInd Dynasty or approximately 1000 B.C.[2] but the evidence is not conclusive. In the absence of anything more definite, we can only look at the problem as it relates to the development of the needle and here the field widens enormously. Bone needles have been found in river caves in the South of France and elsewhere which are of paleolithic origin dating from about 15000 B.C. But whether such needles were used to sew skins together in the accepted sense or whether they were used more after the manner of a bodkin is unclear. The chances are that holes were pierced in the skins with an awl or similar implement and that the needle was merely used to thread sinew through the holes as a means of binding the skins together. If this is correct the introduction of the thimble may not have taken place until the development of spun thread and woven textiles.

Spindle whorls which have been recovered from various sites indicate that spun thread was being produced by 5000 B.C., and as regards woven textiles an early picture of a loom on a Mesopotamian seal and a similar picture on an Egyptian painted dish confirm that cloth was being woven by 3000 B.C. In Egypt flax, which is indigenous to the Nile Valley, was used to make linen garments, and in more northern climates wool was widely used. We can assume therefore that some form of domestic sewing was practised and that the thimble may well have come into being about this time. If so, such a thimble was probably made of leather, a material which was used to make thimbles in Europe until well into medieval times and which is still used in various parts of the Far East. It is known that the Assyrian archers used leather guards to protect their hands and forearms when drawing a bowstring so that it would be logical if thimbles had been made of leather. It would also account for the fact that no early thimbles have survived, because of the perishable nature of leather.

The introduction of bronze which also dates from about 3000 B.C. must have had considerable influence in the development of thimbles. Before the use of bronze, needles were necessarily made of wood, bone (including fish bone) or copper but bronze was an altogether harder and more suitable material with which to make needles. Many of these early bronze needles have been recovered but it is noticeable that the majority are coarse and in most cases it is clear from the thickness of the eye that they were not intended for domestic sewing as we know it today. There must therefore be some doubt as to the exact role which they played and it is possible that it was the introduction of iron and the subsequent development of the steel needle which led to the adoption of the metal thimble. The art of making steel needles was developed in China several centuries before Christ and steel needles reached Asia Minor towards the end of the pre-Christian era. It is tempting to speculate that the leather thimble was not sufficient protection from the harder metal and that the introduction of the bronze thimble came about in consequence. Certainly from a timing point of view the bronze thimble does appear to have been introduced about the same time as the steel needle so that it is not unreasonable to think that the two may be related.

Turning to the British Isles, the history of the thimble is equally obscure. The traditional picture of the early Briton before the arrival of the Romans, clad in skins and painted with woad, is greatly misleading and part of a general misconception that the higher civilisations of the Mediterranean held a monopoly of development. The truth is that the needle and thread had long been in use – bronze needles have been found dating back to about 700 B.C. – and that by the time of the invasion the weaving of textiles was surprisingly well developed. Moreover the two Celtic words 'byswain' meaning a finger guard or shield and 'gwniadur' meaning a sewing steel suggest that the early Britons possessed some form of thimble to protect their finger when sewing. Nevertheless if the early Britons had thimbles, none have survived and the oldest thimbles which have been found in the British Isles would here again appear to be of Roman origin.

The first reference to a thimble (thymel) in the English language – 'Wyrc (th)onne (th)ýmel tó' – arises about 1000 A.D.[3] Eric Partridge's *Short Etymological Dictionary of Modern English* confirms that the word for a thimble originates from the Old English 'thūma', a thumb, from which is derived the word 'thȳmel' and from that 'thimble', the intrusive letter 'b' arriving under the influence of Middle English 'tho(u)mbe' during the fifteenth century. Other forms of the word arose in different parts of the British Isles such as thimal in West Yorkshire, thimel and thimmy in Derbyshire, thimmel in Lothian, Northumberland, Durham and North Lancashire, thimmle in East Yorkshire and thumble in Scotland.

The derivation of the word 'thymel' suggests that the early thimbles were used on the thumb and Brewer's *Dictionary of Phrase and Fable* states that the thimble is so-called because 'it was originally worn on the thumb, as sailors still wear their thimbles'. But is this correct and did sailors wear thimbles – as distinct from the sailors' palm – on their thumbs? To the present-day needlewoman, accustomed to delicate fabrics and fine needles, the idea of wearing a thimble to protect the thumb will seem odd, but going back into the past the needle, as we have seen, was not always the finely polished hardened steel article that we know today. Moreover the materials to be stitched were coarser and included a great deal of leather. Thus the pressure exerted by the tip of the finger would have been insufficient. More pressure can be exerted by the side of the finger, which is the way tailors sew and even more pressure can be exerted with the thumb. A sailor's thimble was described before the British Archeological Association in 1879 (see Bibliography, p. 146). This was made of stout brass, dating probably from the end of the seventeenth century and had been found at Billingsgate a few years previously. The thimble measured one inch and two-twelfths in height and nearly one inch in diameter at the base, and had a circular aperture on the crown a quarter of an inch in diameter. The whole surface of the metal, save a band at the lower part, was covered with ten rows of large pits. Evidently such a thimble, having an open top, was intended to be used sideways like a tailor's thimble but nowadays sailors use what is known as a sailmaker's – or, in the case of saddlers and upholsterers, as a leather worker's – palm. This is not a true thimble but it serves the same purpose, consisting essentially of a bracelet of leather steadied by two openings, one larger to take the four fingers of the hand and the other smaller and rounder for the thumb only. A circle of iron pitted and with a roughened surface fits into the leather and is used to push the needle through the heavy canvas or tanned hide. The advantage of the palm is that it enables the wearer to use the full force of the wrist but clearly the stresses imposed on the needle are enormous and its adoption necessitated the development of needles of suitable strength and design to withstand the force involved.

Somewhat similar considerations probably led to the adoption of the finger rather than the thumb for normal needlework purposes. Early needles being blunt and coarse, the thumb or the side of the finger had to be used in order to achieve sufficient pressure. But with the development of steel needles and also the weaving of lighter fabrics, needlework became a more delicate affair. After the introduction of steel needles from China into Asia Minor, Damascus became a centre for fine needle making and later the Moors brought their skill to Spain which developed a thriving needle industry. Spanish needles were highly prized and it was not until the sixteenth century that the manufacture of steel needles was introduced into England and thence to other parts of Europe. These steel needles, fine and highly polished, necessitated much less pressure to work them through the fabric – no more than would conveniently be exerted with the tip of the finger – and so with the exceptions already noted, thumb sewing or sewing with the side of the finger was abandoned in favour of present-day practice.

The association of the thimble with the thumb is not wholly peculiar to the English language and early French distinguishes between a 'polliceum' (from the Latin 'pollex' meaning a thumb) and a 'deel' (from the Latin 'digitus' meaning a finger). But in most countries the modern word for a thimble is associated with the finger. The French word 'dé' derives from the old French 'deaul' and 'deel' which as already indicated comes from the Latin 'digitus', a finger. This is also the derivation of the Italian 'ditale' and the Spanish 'dedal' which all have the same root. The Swedes call a thimble a 'fingerborg' (borg = castle) with the sense of protection or defence and the Germans more prosaically call a thimble a 'Fingerhut', literally a finger-cap. The Hebrew word is also associated with the finger. Indeed the English word for a thimble might have followed the same derivation for according to the *Dictionary of Needlework* leather thimbles in England were known as fingerlings until the fourteenth century when leather was superseded by metal and the word thimble was adopted. Why the English derivation followed the word for a thumb whereas everywhere else the derivation followed the word for a finger must remain a matter for speculation but it serves as a useful reminder that the design and use of needlework tools has evolved over the years to meet changing conditions and requirements.

Early thimbles

Thimbles of bronze, bone and ivory have been recovered from the sites of Greek and Roman cities and though the exact dates are difficult to establish, they would mostly seem to date from the late Roman era. Gertrude Whiting in her book *Tools and Toys of Stitchery* (New York 1928) illustrates a bronze thimble which was excavated in Syria and said to date from about 300 B.C. but the shape is distinctly Byzantine and the date is unlikely. The oldest known thimbles about whose dates we can be certain are some bronze thimbles open at both ends like tailors' thimbles which were discovered at Herculaneum which was, it will be recalled, destroyed when Vesuvius erupted in A.D. 79 and therefore establishes their date with accuracy. In France metal thimbles have often been found among Gallo-Roman remains and in England a specimen was found at Verulamium (St. Albans) which has been accepted as Roman. The Musée des Antiquités Nationales at St. Germain-en-Laye near Paris has in its safekeeping a number of Roman thimbles including a specimen which might well be a child's thimble, and several other museums, notably the Musée des Antiquités at Rouen, have old thimbles ranging from the time of the Roman conquest to that of the Merovingian dynasty.

1 Roman, Gallo-Roman and other early thimbles and sewing rings from the lower Seine valley.
(*Musée des Antiquités, Rouen*)

There are two main varieties of early thimbles. The first is normally referred to as the ring-type and is similar in concept to the present-day tailor's thimble. It is designed to be used sideways and has the advantage that with an open top, the tip of the finger is exposed and free to assist in picking up pins, needles and thread. All the specimens found at Corinth (perhaps a hundred) were of this variety.

The second is normally referred to as the sugar-loaf type though it might be more appropriate to refer to this variety as the domed type since it includes thimbles of a number of different shapes. Its main feature is that unlike the ring-type, the tip of the finger is covered. The tip may be rounded or flattened bearing indentations like a modern thimble. It may equally be pointed or else smooth without indentations, indicating that the thimble was designed to be used sideways like a tailor's thimble.

To judge from the specimens which have survived, it would seem that Roman thimbles were normally made of cast bronze. The molten bronze was probably poured into a stone mould and allowed to cool, after which the casting would be filed and cleaned and the indentations would be added by hand. Joan Liversidge reminds us however that little sewing was needed for dressmaking during Roman times because pins and brooches usually replaced buttons and button-holes and sometimes shoulder seams.[4] Thus the small number of bronze thimbles which have survived, coupled to the fact that they were often designed to protect the side of the finger rather than the finger-tip, suggests that bronze thimbles may have been intended primarily for heavy work such as sewing hides, leather or sail-cloth material. Lighter thimbles made of bone or ivory may have been reserved for everyday sewing as well of course as thimbles made of leather.

The dating of early metal thimbles presents considerable problems. In a catalogue of the British Museum it is suggested that the more ancient specimens were less finely pitted on the outer surface than those of later date. There is some truth in this proposition when regarded in general terms but there are exceptions and it is not always a reliable guide. The shape of the indentations may sometimes be helpful because it would seem that large triangular and square cut indentations (as well as rounded ones) were used by the Romans and seldom afterwards but here also there are exceptions. The most that can be said is that old thimbles are difficult to date and more often than not the best indications are provided from the location and other circumstances surrounding their discovery.

Leather being perishable, there is as we have seen, little if any direct evidence concerning the use of leather thimbles except in so far as we know about them from early writings and from tradition handed down. By the Middle Ages, the English language distinguished between the leather thimble which was known as a fingerling and the metal thimble which was known as a thymel and is at the origin of the modern word. It is believed that the fingerling consisted of a strip of leather sewn up one side and in its original form it was probably used sideways in the same way as a tailor's thimble. The accompanying illustration shows two such leather thimbles of a type still used in Mongolia which, it will be noticed, are open at both ends. It has sometimes been suggested that leather thimbles had a stitched-on cap but this was probably a later development. Fingerlings were in everyday use during the Middle Ages both in England and on the Continent. In France during the twelfth century servants made use of a leather thimble called a polliceum or digital and in England during the fifteenth century Thomas Hoccleve wrote:

> Come hider to me, sone and look whedir,
> In this purs ther be any croyse or crouche,
> Sauf nedel and threde and themel of leather.[5]

Examples of leather thimbles could still be found in the last century in remote parts of England and in Southern Ireland. It is said that these occasionally found their way into curiosity shops where they masqueraded as Elizabethan. It is hardly necessary to add that it is very unlikely that any of these early leather thimbles survive.

2 Leather ring-type thimbles from Outer Mongolia. *(Private collection)*

Meanwhile, by the Middle Ages the shape and method of manufacture of metal thimbles had evolved. They had become more rounded, they were pitted all over and whilst the heavier thimbles continued to be cast in moulds or else were hammered into shape, lighter thimbles were made in two sections joined together. The domed upper part was either cast or raised from the plate and covered with indentations. The lower part was shaped from the plate and vertically seamed. Such thimbles were normally worn on the thumb. The early history of thimble-making in England is obscure. In France by the thirteenth century there were already two guilds engaged in the manufacture of thimbles, the 'fermaillers' or clasp and buckle makers and the 'boutonniers' or button makers. The workmen engaged in this work were called 'deeliers' or 'deiliers'. Moreover, quality was important: '1260 – Nus du mestier (des frémaillers de laton) dessusd. ne puet faire deux (dés) pour home et pour fame establis à coudre, qui ne soient bons et loyaux, bien marcheans, de bon estoffe, c'est assavoir de bon laton et de fert.'[6] In free translation this may be interpreted: 'No member of the corporation may produce men's and women's thimbles which are not of good and proper quality, well constructed and made of sound materials, that is to say of good quality latten and iron.'

Such thimbles were produced in large quantities and were an accepted part of everyday life. In 1462 François Villon was awaiting execution when he wrote his famous 'Ballade des Pendus' and was moved to picture his own corpse swinging in the wind: 'Plus becquetéz d'oyseaulx que dez à couldre' (More hole-pecked by the birds than a thimble). Clearly Villon who, although he associated with rogues and vagabonds was nevertheless an educated man, would not have used this simile if the pitted metal thimble was not already in everyday use.

In England latten continued to be used until it was eventually superseded by brass proper. There is some confusion regarding the difference between brass and latten, both being an alloy of copper and zinc, and from a thimble collector's point of view they are virtually indistinguishable from each other. Basically the difference is that until the eighteenth century metallic zinc was unavailable so that the foundries used the ores of carbonate and silicate of zinc otherwise known as calamine. Originally therefore latten was composed of unrefined zinc and copper whereas from about 1730 onwards metallic zinc became available and the brass-founding industry was developed on a basis of refined zinc and copper. However during the seventeenth century the word brass was already being applied to articles made of latten so that it can be argued that brass is merely the modern form of the same word. Not many of these early latten (or brass) thimbles have survived but there is a fine collection in the Medieval Department of the London

Museum which is well worth examining by anyone interested in the subject.

Whilst the common people made do with ordinary leather or metal thimbles, it was a natural development that the ladies of the great Courts of Europe should procure finer and costlier needlework tools. Early in the Middle Ages, the urge to decorate and embellish led craftsmen to draw on their artistic powers and already by the fourteenth century French goldsmiths (the term goldsmith was formerly used indiscriminately for both gold- and silversmiths) were making thimbles decorated with the coat-of-arms or the crest of their owners. During the sixteenth century thimbles were decorated with foliated scrolls and ornamental motifs in relief which took the place of the more traditional indentations. At the end of the sixteenth century it became the fashion to embellish thimbles with a short inscription or motto. 'To this gift is joined my kindest thoughts' on a thimble dated 1587 or 'Happiness and love no thief can steal from me' on a thimble dated 1599 are two examples from Germany, whilst in England during Elizabethan times many thimbles were more simply inscribed with the words 'God save the Quene'.

On the Continent during the fifteenth century Milan became a centre for the manufacture of thimbles: '1483 – Une liete de boys blanc, en laquelle a ..., des déaulx de Milan et des esguilles' (Inventory of Queen Charlotte – second wife of Louis XI).

A century later the more costly thimbles were manufactured of gold garnished with precious stones: '1583 – Un petit coffre de cuir noir, là où est dedans deux dés d'or à coudre garnis de rubis (Inventory of the jewels and precious stones of the closet of the King of Navarre).

The importance of the thimble during the sixteenth century is confirmed from Brittany: 'Vous faisant un jour apres une œillade, un soubriz de travers, un coing doeil, ou seulement que vous puissiez toucher sa robbe, ou luy lever son deal, ou fuseau, certes vous estes (ce vous semble) le plus heureux de tout le monde.'[7] This can be translated: 'If one day after you have looked at her she smiles aside or glances at you, or if only you have the opportunity to touch her clothing or to pick up her thimble or her spindle, you are (or so it seems to you) the happiest of all men.'

Apart from providing an amusing commentary on the customs of the age, it will be noted that the thimble is mentioned together with the spindle, confirming the important place which the thimble held in daily life.

The practice of giving a thimble as a present had already lost some of its novelty by the seventeenth century or so one should judge from the following lines: 'It was a happy age when a man might have

3 Sixteenth-century silver
thimble, German inscribed
1577. Height 2·5 cm.
*(Metropolitan Museum of Art,
New York)*

wooed his wench with a pair of kid leather gloves, a silver thimble or with a tawdry lace; but now a velvet gown, a chain of pearl, or a coach with four horses will scarcely serve the turn.'[8]

Certain improvements in thimble-making technique may be noted during the sixteenth century when indentations were first made on a lathe. At first the indentations may have been knurled a single row at a time but soon several knurled wheels were fitted together. The indentations on a number of specimens dated 1580 or thereabouts from the Albert Figdor collection which are illustrated by H. R. d'Allemagne[9] give clear evidence of how the knurled wheels were applied in groups. But such progress as there was proved very slow and the practice of indenting thimbles by hand was to continue for at least another century or more.

The frontispiece showing a sixteenth century thimble-maker is after an engraving by Jost Amman (1539-1591) which appeared in Hartman Schopperum's book *Panoplia omnium illiberalium mechanicarum et sedentarium artium genera continens*, published in Frankfurt-am-Main in

4 Silver thimble, made in two parts: the left-hand portion fits over the right-hand portion in the manner of a cover to protect the engraving. Inscribed Sara Reigersberg 1594.
(Zeeuws Museum, Middelburg)

1564. The engraving was reproduced in *Engentliche Beschreibung aller Stände auff Erden* by Hans Sachsen, 1568, and was accompanied by a few lines of verse:

Der Fingerhüter

> Auss Messing mach ich Fingerhüt
> Blechweiss werden im Feuwer glüt
> Denn in das Ensen glenck getriebn
> Darnach löchlein darein gehiebn
> Gar mancherln art eng und weit
> Für Schuster und Schneider bereit
> Für Seidensticker und Näterin
> Dess Handwercks ich ein Meister bin.

(The Thimble-maker – Out of brass I make thimbles using plate metal. They are tempered by fire, then they are stamped in a die, after which holes are indented: of many sizes, narrow and broad: for cobblers and tailors made, for silk-workers and seamstresses. I am master of this craft.) The engraving appeared in several editions of *Panoplia omnium...* including one published in Frankfurt-am-Main in 1578 from which the present illustration is taken. It shows the artisan in his shop, on the left an apprentice stamps the thimbles into a metal mould and his master, sitting at the work bench in front of him, finishes them by punching the indentations. In order to make the illustrations more intelligible the artist has enlarged the thimbles beyond their proper scale. This

5 Early brass thimbles:
a. Sewing ring – no rim, surface covered by three rows of hand-punched indentations. Found in the City of London. Height 1·0 cm.
b. Sides covered with spiral of hand-punched indentations (8 rows) and crown with separate spiral (3 rows). Found in London Wall. Fifteenth-century. Height 1·7 cm.
c. Sides covered with spiral of machine-made rectangular shaped indentations (6 rows) and crown with separate spiral (3 rows). Found in the City of London. Possibly sixteenth-century. Height 2·2 cm.
d. Sides covered with hand-punched indentations spaced in vertical lines and crown separately indented. Found in the City of London. Possibly sixteenth-century. Height 1·8 cm.
e. Covered with spiral of indentations (9 rows) with top inadequately indented. Found in Westminster. Height 2·1 cm.
f. Covered with spiral of indentations (8 rows), top smooth and square cut. Found in the City of London. Fifteenth- or sixteenth-century. Height 1·8 cm.
g. *(centre thimble)* Indented only on top (lined pattern), the sides decorated with incised foliate ornament. Found with early eighteenth-century objects at 71 Mark Lane in the City of London. Height 1·9 cm.
(Guildhall Museum, London)

type of thimble was evidently made in large quantities and may well have been the same sort which according to G. Bernard Hughes was priced at fourpence a dozen in 1494.[10] He tells us that shops throughout the country stocked them and that the inventory of James Backhouse, a draper in Kirby-in-Lonsdale, taken in 1578, recorded 'Half a hundrethe of thimbles xvj' and 'ij dosen of thimbles xij' – that is, fourpence and sixpence a dozen respectively. This was also the situation in France where shops carried substantial stocks: '1566 – 5 douzaines de daus renforcés 4f.10s.' (Inventory of J. de Cloche, merchant at St. Sever).[11]

The inventories of the fifteenth and sixteenth centuries made frequent reference to thimbles. A silver thimble is mentioned in the will of Dame Philippa Brudenell in 1532; it was bequeathed to the wife of her stepson[12] and in an inventory of the possessions of Queen Elizabeth I there is mention of 'a nedell case of cristall garnysshed with silver gilt with twoo thimbles in it.' The inventory does not mention the material of the thimbles but among the personal possessions of the Queen preserved at Burghley House, Stamford, is a gold thimble, with indentations but without ornament. Another thimble associated with Queen Elizabeth I is made of gold set with rubies and sapphires and is in the Dorothy Howell collection (Plate 5, p. 51). This, according to family tradition, was given by the Queen to her lady-in-waiting and later sold by public auction in London. There are occasional references to thimbles in the work of the writers of the Elizabethan era and two allusions by Shakespeare: Petruchio in *The Taming of the Shrew* (iv, 3) scolds the tailor, 'thou liest, thou thread, thou thimble', and Grumio jeers at him, 'Though thy little finger be armed in a thimble.' Similarly in *King John* (v, 2) the Bastard Faulconbridge says mockingly to the Dauphin:

> For your own ladies and pale-visag'd maids,
> Like Amazons, come tripping after drums,
> Their thimbles into armed gauntlets change,
> Their needles to lances, and their gentle hearts
> To fierce and bloody inclination.

Meanwhile the search for gold had led the Spaniards to the New World where presumably they were the first to introduce the thimble. Certainly we have no evidence of the use of thimbles by North American Indians in pre-colonial times. Thimbles are mentioned in Spanish colonial records as early as 1556: '500 dedales de mujer ... 800 Maravedís', or again, 'Dedales para sastres a rreal y medio la dozena'.[13]

We can assume that the early English settlers also brought thimbles with them. The earliest reference to a thimble which has been traced in this connection dates back to 1649 and relates to the estate of Mr William Whiting '... thimbles, boxes, knives' (Conn. Rec. I 497). We can infer that thimbles became plentiful because they are often found among colonial remains and indeed Ivor Hume goes so far as to say that brass thimbles are among the most common of the smaller domestic objects found on colonial sites.[14] Mr Hume has sought to establish evolutionary trends from the nature and design of the thimbles which have been found but at best this can only be tentative and the subject is fraught with difficulty.

Whilst most of the thimbles used in North America during the seventeenth century were still largely made of brass, the use of silver thimbles by the nobility and gentry in Europe was growing steadily. There are several examples of silver thimbles dating from the sixteenth and seventeenth centuries in the British Museum and in the London

6 Seventeenth-century silver thimbles:
a. *Left*. Chevron design over waffle-shaped indentations. Flower design at top and in a frieze round the rim. Height 2·8 cm.
b. *Right*. Indentations in the form of small circles. Two ovals containing crowned heads. One inscribed C.R.2. (Charles II), the other Q.K. (Catherine of Braganza). Rim Inscribed E.M. Bears maker's mark. Height 2·3 cm. A somewhat similar thimble is in the British Museum collection – see fig. 15.

c. *Left*. Waffle-shaped indentations with looped pattern. Base inscribed 'Feare God and Honour the Kyng'. Height 2·4 cm.
d. *Right*. Indentations in the form of small circles. Base inscribed 'Labour is profitable'. Height 2·7 cm.
(*London Museum*)

Museum but these are rare, due no doubt to the fact that silver thimbles wear out and that until the nineteenth century even a worn or holed thimble retained some value on account of its fine metal content. Thus a silver thimble which was beyond repair was set aside and melted down – a practice which is still current in poorer countries. Moreover in England at the time of the Civil War (1642-1652), a wave of sentiment led the womenfolk on the Parliamentary side to donate their silver thimbles to swell the treasury much in the same way as patriotic English-women donated their aluminium pots and pans during World War II. This is well documented. May wrote that 'The poorer sort, like that widow in the Gospel, presented their Mites also; insomuch that it was common Jeer of men disaffected to the Cause, to call it the Thimble and Bodkin army'[15] and Stephen Daniell echoes him saying that 'the nobles (of Charles I) were profuse in their contributions of plate for the service of the King at Oxford, while on the Parliamentary side, the subscriptions of silver offerings included even such little personal articles as those that suggested the term 'Thimble and Bodkin Army'.[16] Samuel Pepys alludes to it in his Diary for 3rd April, 1663 and Howell (1594-1666) in his *Philanglus* writes that 'the seamstress brought in her silver thimble, the chambermaid her bodkin, the cook her silver spoon.' Popular ballads at the time also tell of the same subject.

In these circumstances it is not perhaps surprising that few silver or gold thimbles have survived from the period prior to the English Civil War. Indeed despite the increasing prosperity of England during the second half of the seventeenth century, authentic specimens of gold and silver thimbles going back much before the end of the eighteenth century are few and far between.

There is surprisingly little pictorial evidence relating to the use of thimbles prior to the eighteenth century with the fortunate exception of some early Dutch paintings: Johannes van der Aack (*c.* 1635-1680), *An old woman seated sewing* (National Gallery – London); Adriaen van Gaesbeeck (1621-1650), *Sewing woman with children* (Staatliche Kunsthalle – Karlsruhe); Egbert van Heemskerk II (1645-1704), *Family portrait of surgeon Jacob Franz Hercules* (Stedelijk Museum – Amsterdam). Dutch painters have an enviable reputation for attention to detail. In all three paintings the women have the thimble clearly shown on their right-hand middle finger and we can conclude that by the end of the seventeenth century the use of the thimble had already been adopted very much as it is today.

7 Silver – probably English or Dutch. Seventeenth-century. Height 2·3 cm.
(*Private collection*)

8 *An old woman seated sewing,* by Johannes van der Aack (*c.* 1635-1680).
(*National Gallery, London*)

Eighteenth-century thimbles

The manufacture of thimbles made of cast brass was introduced into England by John Lofting (or Loftingh), a native of Holland who established himself in London about 1688 as a merchant and manufacturer of fire engines. He became naturalised and in 1693 took out a patent for a machine to make men's, women's and children's thimbles. It is noteworthy that according to the *Encyclopaedia Americana*, the invention of the thimble in Europe was by a Dutchman, Nicholas van Benschoten of Amsterdam. This is evidently misleading though it is known that about 1684 a Dutch goldsmith Nicholas Benschoten acquired some considerable reputation for the manufacture of thimbles. What is more to the point however is that Holland had long been the centre of a thriving thimble-making industry. There are in the archives of the city of Amsterdam many deeds relating to thimbles and thimble manufacturers going back to at least 1600 including a deed dated 28 March 1613 whereby one Babtista van Regemorter who appears to have been a thimble manufacturer from Schoonhoven bought from Jacob Seyne an invention for making thimbles of silver and of brass. It is reasonable to suppose therefore that John Lofting availed himself of a new process unknown in England, and there is some confirmation for this theory in the preamble to his patent which runs as follows:

> WILLIAM & MARY by the grace of God etc ... to all whom these presents come, greeting.
> WHEREAS John Lofting hath, by his humble peticon represented vnto vs the great dutys charged vpon all thimbles imported from beyond the seas doth much discourage the merchants from bringing the same over, soe that the price of that comodity will come to be enhansed vpon our subjects, and that in Germany and other forreigne parts whence they have been heretofore imported into this kingdome, they are vsually made by a certaine engine or instruement hitherto vnknowne in our dominions, and hath humbly prayed vs to grant him our letters of Patents for the sole priviledge of makeing and selling the said engine or instruement,
> KNOW YEE THEREFORE, that wee ...[17]

The reference to an import duty on thimbles and their manufacture in Germany and elsewhere is noteworthy as suggesting that by the end of the seventeenth century thimbles were already the subject of a healthy international trade. It is also interesting to note that Germany has remained an exporter of thimbles to this day.

9 Dutch silver thimble inscribed Ebel Haisma D 1598.
(Fries Museum, Leeuwarden)

Having secured his patent, John Lofting went on to set up a thimble-making works at Islington which was then a village outside London. We know that he arranged for his brother Reynier Loftinck, merchant in Amsterdam, to contract with Pieter Borger, maker of thimbles in Utrecht, for Pieter Borger's eighteen-year-old son Laurens to come to London and to work for Lofting in the making of sewing rings *(naairingen)* and brass thimbles for a period of six years. We are fortunate that a full description of this factory and its method of operation was given by John Houghton F.R.S. writing in July 1697 as follows:

Now for thimbles, which were all brought from Holland, till lately my good friend Mr. John Lofting, a merchant in Bow churchyard, London, a Dutchman, set up the trade at Islington, next door to Young's Wells, and got a patent for it, Anno 1695. There, he made them as follows, with brass:

Which must be of fine metal; for the candlesticks and ordinary metal is brittle; therefore none will do but such as will bear the hammer: Therefore battry or kettle; but the new being 8 pounds the hundred, they cannot afford it: Therefore they will take Shruff, worth about 4 pounds the hundred, which shruff is old hammered brass.

This they melt and cast in a sort of sand, gotten only at Highgate, with which and red-okre are made mould and cores, and in them they usually cast six gross at a cast, and about six or seven of these casts in a day. They are cast in double-rows, and when cold taken out and cut off with greasy shears.

Then boys take out the cores from the inside with a pointed piece of iron, which cores were made by them, every core having a nail with a broad head in it, which head keeps it from the mould, and makes the hollow to cast it in.

This done, they are put into a barrel as they do shot, and turn'd round with a horse, till they rub the sand one from another.

Thus far, the foundery, in which are employ'd six persons: first, the founder and two men make the moulds ready. Secondly, two boys make core, for each thimble one. Thirdly, one that blows the bellows. From hence they are carried to the mill to be turned.

First, the inside, which works with an instrument to the bottom, while 'tis held lasts, and flies back when let loose. Secondly, the outside, which with a coarser engine called a rough turning is made pretty smooth at one stroke; and afterwards, with a finer engine both the side and the bottom are at one stroke made very smooth.

Then some saw-dust or filings of horn-combs are put half-way
into each thimble and upon it an iron punch, and then with
one blow against a studded steed the hollow of the bottom is
made.

After this with an engine the sides have the hollow made, and
in this engine is their chief secret, and they can work off with
it thirty or forty gross in a day.

This done, they are again polished on the inside.

Then the rim with a single or double rib are turn'd at one stroke
and all these turnings are performed with five men and three
boys.

After this, they are again turned in the barrel with saw-dust or
bran to scour them very bright, and so they are compleat .
thimbles.

Thus finished, they are sorted, and put six together one in
another; and six of these sixes are wrapt up in a blue paper,
and four of these papers making a gross, are wrapt up in another
blue or brown paper, and are sold by the first maker at four
or five shillings the gross.

The charge of this work per annum is much about 700 pounds
and there has been made one week with another about 140 gross
which makes 7280 gross or 1048320 thimbles, which at 4 shillings
the gross amounts to 1456 pounds. Out of this a great deal for
the shruff 'tis made on, and a gross of thimbles weigh about
24 or 28 ounces.

He has lately removed his horse-mill at Islington to make it a
watermill at Marlow on the Thames in Buckinghamshire where
with the same mill he can make twice as many thimbles, he also
grinds all sorts of feeds for oil at the same time.[18]

It is not known what prompted John Lofting's removal to Marlow
and he may have met with business difficulties about this time. Possibly
John Lofting was induced to come to Marlow owing to the existence
there of a mill where it is said the manufacture of thimbles had been
carried on ever since the time of Henry VIII.[19] Certainly the nearby
Temple Mills had long been used for the manufacture of metal work,
especially brass and copper, and he may have chosen this site because
of its convenience as regards raw material supplies. Daniel Defoe who
visited Marlow some time after the South Sea Bubble (1721) wrote
as follows:

On the river of Thames, just by the side of this town (Great
Marlow), though on the other bank, are three very remarkable

mills, which are called the Temple-Mills and are called also the Brass Mills, and are for making Bisharn Abbey Battery Work, as they call it, viz. brass kettles, and pans, of all sorts. They have first a foundary, where, by the help of lapis caliminaris, they convert copper into brass, and then, having cast the brass in large broad plates, they beat them out by force of great hammers, wrought by the water mills into what shape they think fit for sale.

Next to these are two mills, both extraordinary in themselves, one for making thimbles, a work excellently well finished, and which performs to admiration, and another for pressing of oyl from rape-seed and flax-seed, both which, as I was told turn to very good account to the proprietors.[20]

The reference to John Lofting's mill is unmistakable and in his will dated 1733 the property listed included two thimble mills. John Lofting died in 1742 leaving seven sons, one of whom founded a charity for the poor of Great Marlow.

Meanwhile by the seventeenth century silver thimbles as distinct from brass or other base metals had come into general use among the middle classes both in England and on the Continent. In France Blois, which was already well-known for its watches, became a centre for the manufacture of fine thimbles, both the round domed type and the open-topped tailors' thimbles. In the inventory of Claudine Bouzonnet Stella (Paris 1693) are mentioned no less than three silver thimbles. Gold thimbles also became popular and some very fine specimens were produced in France where the technique of embellishing thimbles with multi-coloured gold was developed with considerable effect.

The practice of giving a thimble as a present remained very much in evidence. In 1663, James Dillon, later to become Lord Roscommon, returned from a visit to the Verney family at Claydon and sent a gift of two thimbles to Mary Verney and her cousin Doll Leeke, 'that the one should not hurt a fine finger by the making of handkerchiefs, nor the other receive a prick in working my lady's buttons.' Whether these thimbles were made of silver is not stated but the likelihood is that they were and that the recipients were suitably grateful.

Similarly, the large amount of domestic sewing which was necessary in former centuries resulted in a thimble being generally part of a bride's trousseau. This was often a present from her fiancé and would carry a suitable inscription or line of verse. 'Forget-me-not', 'Blessings attend you', 'A keepsake', 'A token of regard' are among the phrases of thimble literature. This custom was to continue well into the nineteenth century.

10 Eighteenth-century French gold thimble ornamented with garland of green gold. Height 2·4 cm.
(Private collection)

11 Silver filigree work, English, eighteenth-century. Height 2·1 cm.
(Private collection)

12 Gold thimble with original galuchat holder. French, late eighteenth-century. Height 2·2 cm.
(Private collection)

Although the use of silver thimbles was increasing, nevertheless the vast majority of household thimbles continued to be made of brass and being in constant use wore out quickly. In the towns, thimbles could be purchased from the mercers who appear to have stocked them in considerable quantities but in the countryside they could be obtained from pedlars or itinerant vendors who traded objects of this kind, or at country fairs. More expensive thimbles might be obtained from toy-sellers as were called shop-keepers specialising in the sale of novelties. Among a list of objects stocked by a Holborn toy-seller 'at the Green Parrot near Chancery Lane' in 1762 were 'steel topt and other thimbles'. Still more expensive thimbles – such as gold or jewelled thimbles – would have been available from a goldsmith.

Also about this time it became the practice in the small boys' and girls' village schools which were known as dame-schools, for the teacher or dame to rap inattentive or naughty children on the head with her thimble-covered finger. This punishment was known as 'thimmel-pie' or 'thimmy-pie' making, and the thimble itself was referred to as 'dame's thimell': 'Missus pullin me ears, broddin me with knittin needle and givin me sa mich thimal-pie'.[21] The practice was apparently not confined to England. It is reported that one of the exhibitors at the French Industrial Products Exhibition in Paris in 1823, Messrs Delaporte Frères, showed tailors' thimbles known as 'verges de fer' – a clear allusion to the use of thimbles for corporal punishment.

Throughout this period the thimble retained considerable importance for sailors because of the tremendous amount of sewing associated with sail-making and the upkeep of sails and canvas generally. The sailmakers' palm does not appear to have been in use and sailors commonly wore their thimbles on the thumb. Sailors' thimbles have occasionally been recovered from harbours, having probably dropped overboard, and they have also been recovered from wrecks such as that of the Spanish ship *El Matancero* which left Cadiz bound for the West Indies at the end of 1740 and went aground 22 February 1741. The wreck was thoroughly investigated in 1959 and among the many articles recovered were several thimbles.[22]

Shortly after the English Civil War a new metal alloy is said to have been invented by Prince Rupert of Bavaria, grandson of James I of England, which came to be known as Prince's metal. This was more coppery than brass to look at and is stated variously to have been an alloy of copper and arsenic or copper and bismuth. The name of Prince's metal also came to be attached to brass with a copper content in the range of 75 to 85 per cent. An example of a thimble made of Prince's metal is described in the Journal of the British Archeological Association, 'The slightly domed top is smooth, with a ring round

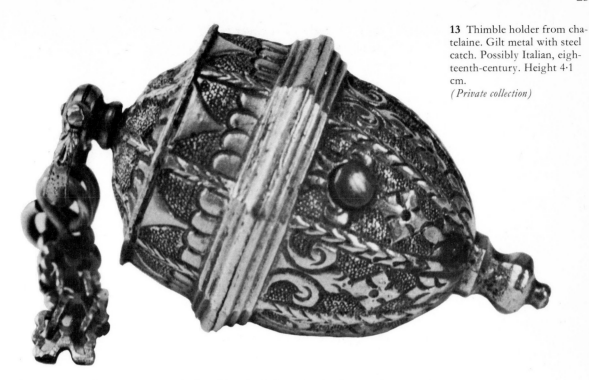

its margin; the upper part of the sides is indented, the lower decorated with a scroll pattern, and there is a trifling rim at the base. This thimble is really a tasteful little thing in its way.'

Prince's metal should not be confused with pinchbeck which is an alloy of five parts copper and one part zinc. It was invented by Christopher Pinchbeck (1670-1732) and was used as a low-priced substitute for gold. During the eighteenth century pinchbeck was used for making thimbles sometimes with a steel top to give added strength and its use was continued well into the nineteenth century. In 1766 Benjamin Halsted, a New York silversmith, advertised thimbles of pinchbeck with steel tops (as well as thimbles of gold and silver) but it is not clear whether they were made in America or whether they were imported.

Less certain is the use of Sheffield plate as invented by Thomas Bolsover in the 1740s and consisting of silver and copper fused and hammered or rolled together. Reports that Bolsover started by making small articles including thimbles[23] remain unconfirmed. On the contrary it would seem that technically it would be difficult to apply the indentations without damaging the thin silver surface and moreover that such surface would not resist the wear of the needle. There is reason to believe therefore that even if Bolsover may have experimented with thimbles, these were never produced commercially.

The introduction of Sheffield plate was followed soon after by the development of Britannia metal, an alloy of 80 per cent or more tin, 5 per cent or more antimony and 1 per cent copper. Thimbles may have been made of Britannia metal but no specimens have yet been recorded.

Meanwhile various technical developments came to revolutionise the manufacture of thimbles at the end of the eighteenth century. As we have seen, indentations were already being knurled several rows at a time by the end of the sixteenth century, but this only applied to a limited range of thimbles and until the latter part of the eighteenth century most thimbles still had the indentations punched individually by hand. Moreover, until the second half of the eighteenth century most thimbles were either cast and worked on a lathe or else built up in two pieces with a rounded dome attached to a seamed body. With the turn of the century new methods of manufacture were introduced and silver thimbles began to be made in one piece by pressing into shape from a blank piece of silver sheeting and then working on a lathe much as silver thimbles are manufactured today.

The above changes in manufacturing technique are an important guide to collectors seeking to date thimbles of English or continental manufacture. Specimens with hand-punched indentations can reasonably be assigned to the eighteenth century or earlier, whereas specimens with machine-made indentations date from the late eighteenth century or more commonly from the nineteenth century or later. In some parts of the world thimbles are still manufactured individually by hand and bear hand-punched indentations. India is a case in point but such thimbles can normally be recognised by their style and need not therefore cause any confusion.

14 English silver thimbles from the eighteenth century. *(Private collection)*

The other guide to dating English thimbles should be the hall-marks, which would normally be found on articles of gold and silver. But this is not the case because the Plate Offences Act of 1738 (described as an Act for the Better Preventing of Frauds and Abuses in Gold and Silver ware), specifically exempted thimbles from hallmarking in common with other objects weighing less than ten pennyweight. This situation was maintained until the Act of 1790 which reduced the exemption limit to only five pennyweight (about eight grams). As most thimbles weigh less than this amount it made no difference and although

15 *Top Row*
a. Silver – no top and flattened. Chevron pattern on side. Rim inscribed 'A Gloriam Deo'. Height 1·6 cm.
b. Brass – from Winchester. Hand-punched indentations. Hole at top. Height 1·3 cm.
c. Brass sewing ring – has engraving of an eagle with wings displayed. Rim inscribed 'Dio Sopra el Tuto'. Italian. Height 1·6 cm.
Middle Row
a. Bronze – hand-punched indentations. Height 2·2 cm.
b. Brass – from Brettenham Norfolk. Cross-hatched with alternate oval and lozenge design. Inscribed H.A.V. English, seventeenth-century. Height 2·6 cm.
c. Silver – from Yorkshire. Damaged at top. Rim inscribed but only part legible: '... avec tout' in Gothic script against silver gilt background.
Bottom Row
a. Silver – commemorative thimble to mark Great Exhibition. Inscribed 'Exhibition of all Nations'. English, 1851. Height 2·6 cm.
b. Bronze – from Herpes, Charente (S.W. France). Beehive shaped thimble with smooth top for sideways sewing with the thumb. Hand-punched indentations. Punched wavy line round the base. Probably Gallo-Roman. Height 2·3 cm.
c. Silver – indentations in the form of small circles. Two ovals, each containing a head. One crowned and inscribed C.R.2. (Charles II). The other obliterated but inscribed Q.K. (Catherine of Braganza). English, seventeenth-century. Height 1·8 cm.
(British Museum)

16 Collection of porcelain, enamel and gold thimbles:

1. Gold thimble holder from a chatelaine. Early eighteenth century.

2. Gold – red gold ornamented with a frieze of foliage and another of flowers in green gold. French, late eighteenth-century.

3. Gold – oval medallions showing naked children playing sundry musical instruments. Eighteenth-century.

4. Gold – unusually long thimble ornamented with two garlands of flowers in golds of different colours. Inscribed M.D. French, nineteenth-century.

5. Silver – decorated with mouldings and facets. Traces of gilding. Inscribed D.E. Seventeenth-century.

6. Gold – two friezes and a shield inscribed L.D. French, nineteenth-century.

7. Porcelain – decorated with birds and foliage. Possibly English, nineteenth-century.

8. Mother-of-pearl – decorated with a double collar of gilt metal. French, early nineteenth-century.

9. Gold – red gold ornamented with foliated scroll in green gold. French, nineteenth-century.

10. Porcelain – roses and green leaves between two narrow bands of gold. Nineteenth-century.

11. Porcelain – large bouquet of pansies between two bands of gold. Nineteenth century.

12. Gold – red gold decorated with green gold. Nineteenth-century.

13. Gold – red gold with a garland of green gold and a small shield. Nineteenth-century.

14. Porcelain – a garland of flowers. Probably nineteenth-century.

(Continued on page 30)

small articles of this kind could be sent for marking if the manufacturers desired it, they did not do so because of the duty. Thus English thimbles remained unmarked until about 1890 when the duty was withdrawn and manufacturers began to send their thimbles to the assay office. Moreover, about the same time English thimble manufacturers who had been content to make thimbles in only three sizes, girls', maids' and women's, began to follow the example of the United States by offering their thimbles in a range of numbered sizes. Since then the practice has become universal and few, if any, modern English gold or silver thimbles are sold without both a hallmark and a size number.

It follows therefore that the older thimbles are usually those without marks of any sort except possibly a maker's mark, whereas a thimble which is hallmarked or which has a size number is likely to be less than a hundred years old.

The absence of hallmarks on the older thimbles makes it difficult to date them with accuracy. The collector is thrown back on style, patina and method of manufacture and as in all branches of antique collecting, experience is the determining factor. In practice most of the older thimbles finding their way into collectors' hands are likely to have been manufactured during the nineteenth century when, because of the rapid increase in population and higher standards of living, both the quantity of thimbles and the variety available increased enormously. The accompanying illustrations show many fine specimens with a few brief notes bringing out the salient points. A study of these illustrations will serve better than any amount of description to improve the reader's knowledge and at the same time will underline the tremendous amount of care and ingenuity which our ancestors devoted towards improving and embellishing their humblest possessions.

17 The Colonial Williamsburg Foundation have been fortunate enough to acquire a fine collection of thimbles including some rare items and so far as is known it is the only museum in the world possessing a representative collection of this kind.
Top Row (left to right)
English porcelain, Derby (marked), about 1870.
English porcelain, Royal Worcester (marked), twentieth-century.
Germany, silver with cornelian stone top. Late nineteenth-century.
English silver filigree about 1830.
Enamel thimble of unknown origin. Late eighteenth- or early nineteenth-century.
Bottom row (left to right)
English gold and tortoiseshell. Piercy's patent about 1815.
Vegetable ivory (corozo nut), English, about 1850.
French mother-of-pearl. Palais Royal, about 1815.
Unusual ivory thimble, Indian or Chinese, made for European market probably about 1850.
Glass thimble, probably nineteenth-century.
(Colonial Williamsburg Foundation)

Porcelain thimbles

Porcelain thimbles are the aristocrats of any thimble collection and are available in so many beautiful and colourful designs that some collectors specialise in them and nothing else.

The manufacture of porcelain thimbles appears to have its origins on the Continent where they were produced during the eighteenth century by several factories, notably Meissen. Being very delicate, few of these early thimbles have survived and specimens can command high prices. The highest price yet recorded for a thimble was 1,500 guineas (3,750 dollars) which was paid at Christie's in 1969 for a fine early eighteenth century Meissen thimble. This thimble, which was made at the famous Hoeroldt workshop, is decorated around the base with a miniature harbour scene showing six ships, thirty figures and a variety of merchandise all in perfect and exquisite detail. Although this price was exceptional, it is not uncommon for eighteenth-century continental porcelain thimbles in·good condition to fetch 1,000 dollars or more. Occasional specimens may still turn up, but most surviving eighteenth-century thimbles have found their way into private collections and the vast majority of the porcelain thimbles which are still about date from the nineteenth century or later.

Early porcelain thimbles are seldom marked and are therefore extremely difficult to attribute to their factory of manufacture. Moreover, during the eighteenth century it was the practice of some factories to make plain undecorated thimbles which were subsequently decorated by the factory itself or by outside decorators according to the demand so that it is difficult to establish any given pattern. Sometimes the origin of a thimble is unmistakable. There is, for instance, a very fine specimen from the Mennecy-Villeroy (Essone) factory (1734-73) at the Musée National de Céramique in Paris which is so typical of this factory's work as regards the paste, the colouring and the design that any other attribution is unthinkable. But more often than not there is little to go by and· the situation is further complicated because there is still a great deal of doubt as to which factories actually made thimbles. Sèvres, for instance, has been mentioned occasionally by collectors who came across a porcelain thimble bearing an inscription in French, but the truth is that a thimble of this nature is more likely to have been manufactured in Germany where, during the eighteenth century, French was considered to be the language of elegance and refinement. The Sèvres records are not necessarily complete so that it is not possible to be absolutely certain, but the available evidence, particularly with regard to the eighteenth century, is that Sèvres did not make thimbles.

It is impossible to do justice to the variety of porcelain thimbles

(Continuation from page 28)

15. Porcelain – roses between two borders of gold. Nineteenth-century.
16. Silver – wire work decorated with foliage and four leaves in blue and green enamel. Far East, eighteenth-century.
17. Gold – in the shape of a tiara set with rubies. Oriental, sixteenth-century.
18. Steel scissors with gold inlay. Sino-Persian, early seventeenth-century.
19. Enamel – hand-painted with a posy of flowers and inscribed 'Traue Nicht es Schticht' (Be careful, it stings). Late eighteenth-century.
20. Enamel – hand-painted flowers on white ground. English, late eighteenth-century.
21. Gold with a silver enamel surround. Inscribed 'Qui de cœur aime, de bon cœur donne' (He who loves, gives willingly) and the initials E.I. At the top of the thimble there is a coat of arms under glass showing a fleur de lys half gold and half black stamped with a helmet. The silver surround shows foliage in blue enamel on which are mounted small yellow and pink flowers. French, sixteenth-century.
22. Porcelain – a band of flowers very finely painted. Late eighteenth-century.
23. Porcelain – a narrow band of red flowers interspersed with green leaves. Late eighteenth-century.

(Albert Figdor collection)

which were made in Germany and neighbouring countries during the eighteenth century. Suffice it to say that almost every style of porcelain decoration may be found, be it landscapes, pastoral scenes, fishing or hunting scenes, chinoiseries, harlequinades, flower or bird motifs, silhouettes, etc. (Plate 4, p. 50). The thimbles themselves normally have a rounded top which is indented and the design is painted in miniature round the sides. A typical feature is that instead of a straight rim the thimbles may have a rim which is cut away in scallops or else crenellated. It is tempting to describe all thimbles of this kind as Meissen, if only because of the difficulty of attributing the thimbles to the right factory of origin, but this should be resisted. That Meissen made thimbles is incontrovertible because Meissen was one of the few factories which troubled to mark thimbles. A specimen is described above and there is another Meissen thimble in the collection of the Museum für Kunst und Gewerbe at Hamburg. This thimble bears the crossed-swords mark of Meissen in underglaze blue on the inside and it is decorated round the outside with a harbour scene in the style of Johann Gregorius Hoeroldt suggesting that it was probably made about 1740 (Plate 3, p. 49). These are obviously Meissen, but there are others of different shapes and styles which almost certainly originated elsewhere. For instance, it is known that the Fürstenberg factory made thimbles because in a list of the Fürstenberg factory's products dated 1769, thimbles are mentioned under the heading of 'galenterien'.[24] Similarly Nymphenburg were probably making thimbles at about the same time because a pattern book dated 1767 includes the design for a thimble.[25] No doubt other German factories, as well as the Vienna factory, made thimbles, but the evidence is no longer available.

The fashion for porcelain thimbles was not confined to Germany and several of the continental factories are known to have made them. From a price list dated 1769, of the Swiss factory at Schooren near Zurich, we know that the Schooren factory made thimbles and that plain ones were sold at 18 kreuzers and decorated ones at 50 kreuzers.[26] There is no evidence that the other Swiss factory at Nyon (1781-1813) on the lake of Geneva made thimbles but since Nyon produced other needlework items such as knitting-needle protectors, it is by no means improbable.

In France, as we have seen, Mennecy made thimbles and the Musée de Sèvres owns a thimble which is believed to be old Paris porcelain. This is unmarked and is decorated round the base with a frieze of flowers and a band of gold. An unusual feature is that the thimble is painted blue on the inside. Somewhat better documented are Danish thimbles from the Royal Copenhagen Porcelain Manufactory whose order book for 1778 includes about a dozen thimbles of various kinds, amongst them plain thimbles, thimbles decorated in purple enamel or thimbles gilt with name.[27] A works list dated 1779 also refers to purple enamel. There is a Copenhagen porcelain thimble in the collection of the Museum of Decorative Art at Copenhagen and two in the Royal Porcelain Factory's own collection, besides others in private hands.

Finally, the 'Duca di Martina' museum in the Villa Floridiana at Naples owns an enamelled thimble-case with gold mounts containing a small porcelain thimble which is attributed to the Royal factory of Naples (1771-1806). No doubt thimbles were also made in other continental factories not mentioned above but thimbles were regarded as such trifles that the factories seldom bothered to mention or list them separately and the evidence is therefore elusive.

In England soft paste thimbles are known to have been produced by the Chelsea and the Worcester factories. Among other evidence, extracts from the Chelsea factory weekly bills for the period 1770 to 1773 include one item '96 thimbles, painted overtime by Boardman & Co. £0.12.0', in other words one-and-a-half pence per thimble for the cost of decoration.[28] There is an attractive specimen (though, unfortunately, it has had to be repaired) in the Victoria and Albert Museum in London. Part of the famous Schreiber collection, it is ascribed to Chelsea, about 1765, on grounds of material and style of painting. Similarly, the Worcester Royal Porcelain Company's records show that from 1790 onwards Worcester were receiving orders for cyphered thimbles or thimbles with initials as specified either for individual orders or for gifts. The price was about eighteen pence. On the other hand there is some doubt whether thimbles were produced at the Derby factory during the eighteenth century. Derby frequently modelled its wares on other factories, notably Chelsea, so that there is room for confusion. We do know that in the 'list of moulds and models which belonged to the estate of the late Mr Duesbury in 1795, as estimated by Messrs Soar, Longden, Farnsworth and Hardenburg' one of the entries reads 'Eight thimbles'.[29] Duesbury was proprietor of the Derby factory so that there is a strong likelihood that they came from Derby but one cannot be sure.

It is not however until the second quarter of the nineteenth century that thimbles of bone china, strong and tough compared to the earlier soft paste specimens, began to be produced in quantity. Among the wide range which were made are those of the Coalport, Derby, Minton, Rockingham and Worcester factories which all engaged in the manufacture of bone china thimbles. Enquiries from the Spode factory suggest that Spode/Copeland did not make thimbles and similarly the Royal Doulton group state that there is no reference to porcelain thimbles in the Doulton records. Such thimbles were normally made of plain china with delicate designs of birds and flowers, and sometimes included initials and other ornamental decoration. The thimbles are glazed inside and out though usually the glazing is omitted from the tip of the thimble leaving the indentations rougher than if they were glazed over and thus providing a better grip for the head of the needle. Nineteenth-century thimbles are seldom marked, but later examples have been noted bearing the Minton, Derby, Royal Worcester and Royal Crown Derby marks.

Among English nineteenth-century porcelain thimbles the most frequently encountered are those of the Worcester factory. Although unmarked, Worcester thimbles of this period are readily recognisable by their shape and by the distinctive Worcester paste well known to porcelain collectors. Mid-nineteenth-century Worcester thimbles are characterised by hand-painted birds or similar designs and by delicately traced and ornamented gilt edging. Plain thimbles may also be decorated with a glass-like beading. Towards the end of the century the design grows plainer and heavier. Thimbles of so-called 'creamware' or 'biscuit' Worcester, decorated with birds and flowers on a cream background, were made from about 1890 till 1910.

18 Worcester porcelain thimbles, nineteenth-century. *(Private collection)*

19 Worcester porcelain thimbles with bird designs painted by William Powell and bearing his signature. Twentieth-century.
(Private collection)

20 Modern Royal Worcester porcelain thimble. Printed design.
(Private collection)

21 Derby porcelain thimble (marked), about 1870.
(Private collection)

Later examples usually bear the Royal Worcester mark applied in purple coloured transfer and include a date mark which is incorporated into the factory mark by means of an elaborate system of dots and symbols. Those marked 'Royal Worcester England' date from about 1900 to about 1928 and those marked 'Royal Worcester – Made in England' from about 1928 to 1963 when the dating system was abandoned on thimbles. One charming series produced during the inter-war years was decorated by William Powell who worked at the Royal Worcester factory from 1900 to 1950. William Powell specialised in British bird subjects and flowers. He was a hunchback and dwarf but in spite of this he was an outstandingly contented and cheerful man whose personality is well reflected in his work. He painted with considerable perception and there is little doubt that thimbles and indeed any porcelain bearing his signature will be increasingly sought after. Royal Worcester still make porcelain thimbles hand-decorated with birds, flowers and fruit and each bears the signature of the artist. Since 1963 such thimbles bear the factory mark in black transfer with the letter R in a circle underneath. Being relatively inexpensive, they are in great demand and the Royal Worcester factory produces them in surprising quantities. Besides hand-decorated thimbles, Royal Worcester also make thimbles decorated with a lithoprint but these are not signed. Royal Adderley (a member of the Doulton group) are the only other English factory still making thimbles but their designs are all printed to the exclusion of hand-decoration. The success of the Royal Worcester thimbles may have prompted the Hungarian porcelain factory at Herend to follow suit and the latter now produce somewhat similar hand-painted thimbles with floral designs.

Reverting to the nineteenth century, Derby thimbles are relatively scarce compared to Worcester, and specimens sometimes featuring birds or butterflies are sought after. Some later specimens from the King Street factory bear the Stevenson and Hancock mark indicating that they were manufactured some time after 1862. There is a typical example of an S and H thimble in the Derby Museum collection, painted with a rose, pansy and forget-me-not. Such thimbles occasionally come up for auction: 'Derby thimble, attractively painted with a robin perching in a leafy green branch, above double gilt border, one inch' is a typical entry. This thimble was sold for £45 during the 1970-71 season. Coalport thimbles are also scarce and in the absence of marks difficult to identify. They too may come up for auction: 'an attractive Worcester thimble of small size painted with a robin on honeysuckle, gilt dot and scroll borders, 3/4 inch, and a Coalport thimble with a boldly coloured bird on a leafy branch, 3/4 inch'. This pair was sold for £115 during the 1972-73 season.

Porcelain thimbles sometimes carry an inscription which may provide a clue to their origin. During the eighteenth century porcelain thimbles often bore a short motto such as 'Gage de mon amitié,' 'L'amitié me garde', 'Fidélité toujours', 'Mon feu (ma flamme) durera toujours', 'Avec le temps', etc. These and other inscriptions will normally be found in French but, as already mentioned, do not necessarily denote that the thimble is of French manufacture. Other thimbles may bear the initials or cypher of their owner which was a common practice at the end of the eighteenth century. Or again during the nineteenth century, a porcelain thimble might bear a local reference such as a thimble inscribed 'I thought of you in Meissen' in German and a Worcester thimble dating from about 1850 which bears the inscription 'A present from Towyn'.

A feature of eighteenth- and nineteenth-century porcelain thimbles is that more often than not they are relatively small, too small and narrow to fit on a normal finger. Possibly the average person is larger than was the case a hundred and fifty or two hundred years ago and moreover a lady of quality such as was likely to own a porcelain thimble was not expected to do manual work so that her fingers were likely to remain slimmer. Nevertheless, even if these factors are taken into account, porcelain thimbles do tend to be abnormally small, a feature which is probably related to their fragility. The life of a porcelain thimble in everyday use was likely to be limited, but if a porcelain thimble was otherwise too small to wear, it tended to be put aside where it had a better chance to survive unharmed. This feature does

22 Modern porcelain and earthenware thimbles and thimble shapes.
(Private collection)

not apply only to porcelain thimbles. The smaller silver thimbles are almost invariably better preserved than the large ones. The difference between porcelain and silver, however, is that the larger silver thimbles tend to be worn and damaged whereas in the case of porcelain, once broken the thimbles were a total loss and this is reflected in the size of those which have survived.

The vogue for thimble collecting and the rarity of porcelain thimbles have encouraged a number of small contemporary artisan factories to make porcelain thimbles of a kind which are not intended for sewing but are directed specifically at collectors. Some of these are very crude but others, notably some of those made in the United States, are decorated with skill, one such series being the bisque thimbles, as they are called, hand-painted and signed by the American artist Mildred Kohls, which are quite tasteful in their own way. Another item in the same category comes from Limoges in France. The design is printed and although shaped like a thimble, there are no indentations. Or again, the English firm Hammersley make an attractive thimble shape decorated with flower patterns but with small pimples instead of indentations. Provided such porcelain thimbles and thimble shapes are accepted for what they are and not passed off as valuable items, no harm need arise and one or two well selected items may even lend colour to a collection when older and rarer items are unavailable.

Porcelain thimbles were often sold in a plain thimble case somewhat similar to the thimble cases in which gold thimbles were normally sold but necessarily somewhat larger and rather ungainly. These are of little interest. Of more consequence are porcelain thimble stands such as, for instance, a Dresden model of a girl carrying the support for a thimble in her hands and wearing a turban-like headgear made of fabric to be used as a pincushion. These thimble stands are comparatively rare and much sought after.

At one time or another pottery manufacturers have produced almost every article which was ever made of porcelain and this includes thimbles. There is a specimen of an earthenware thimble in the Stoke-on-Trent Museum in England whose origins are unknown, but such specimens are uncommon. Possibly earthenware thimbles proved too soft and easily damaged in wear. It has been pointed out that earthenware can be baked at very high temperatures and that, treated in this way and then glazed, it would be neither too soft nor too brittle; but, be that as it may, few earthenware thimbles have survived and the specimen in the Stoke-on-Trent Museum is a rarity. Contemporary earthenware thimbles have recently been offered for sale but these are not genuinely intended for sewing and are directed essentially at collectors.

Enamel thimbles

Enamel as a means of decoration was already well established during the Middle Ages and there is every reason to believe that enamel was used to decorate thimbles by the fourteenth century or earlier. However, so far as is known, none of these older thimbles have survived and the earliest enamel thimbles on record are attributed to the sixteenth century. One is a French gold thimble with an enamelled silver skirting and another is a Persian gold thimble with two miniature enamel portraits surrounded by flowered branches. Unfortunately, enamel thimbles are easily damaged which is probably the reason why early enamel thimbles are very scarce.

Towards the end of the eighteenth century thimbles of painted enamel were produced in England in relatively large quantities. The top only of these thimbles was indented and the sides reserved for decoration. Some examples have a fitted brass cap bearing the indentations as this was stronger and could better resist the wear of the needle than the thin shell of copper which was used as a base for the enamel. These thimbles were made in South Staffordshire (Bilston) from about 1770 and are decorated with posies of flowers on a white ground or with a miniature landscape in a cartouche set against a coloured ground. More rarely they may be decorated with a miniature portrait. Sometimes the thimble serves the dual purpose of acting as a cap for an enamel needle case or else it may be supplied with an egg-shaped thimble case also of painted enamel to match. There are four fine Bilston

Plate 1 *(opposite)* Display of thimbles from the Dorothy Howell collection.

23 Enamel – at left, painted landscape in cartouche on white ground; at right, similar landscape on turquoise ground. English, South Staffordshire (Bilston), eighteenth-century. Height 1·9 cm.
(Private collection)

enamel thimbles in the Schreiber collection at the Victoria and Albert Museum in London (Plate 3, p. 49). Good examples of eighteenth-century English painted enamel thimbles are hard to find and when they do reach the market command high prices.

The art of enamelling has always been very advanced in Russia where it had a long tradition. Some beautiful thimbles were produced and the thimble illustrated in the colour plates is a good example of Russian enamel at its best. It was made by the well-known enameller Ovcinnikov who worked from about 1880 to 1914. Enamel thimbles were very popular and several specimens of lesser quality (rougher design, fewer colours) are also illustrated. The splendours of Russian enamel evoke the name of Fabergé but so far as can be determined no Fabergé thimble was ever made. Some enamel thimbles have been produced in Russia since the Revolution but the work is coarse and of little artistic value.

Norway is another country which has produced enamel thimbles and where during the nineteenth century some very beautiful thimbles were made. Norwegian thimbles are easily recognised from the style and also because they are usually fitted with a moonstone top. The older and finer thimbles are decorated in traditional design in shades

24 Russian enamel thimbles, about 1900.
(Private collection)

Plate 2 *(opposite, above)* Silver thimbles from India, late nineteenth-century.
(Private collection)
(below, left) Thimble-holders from chatelaines (late nineteenth-century) and a thimble stand in the shape of a basket (early nineteenth-century).
(Private collection)
(below, right) Filigree toys combining thimble, scent bottle, tape measure and, at right, a letter seal. English, early nineteenth-century.
(Private collection)

of blue or green enamel with white beading. Later thimbles may be plain with pale yellow, pale blue or light mauve transparent enamel over a guilloche. Another series is decorated with reindeers, snow scenes, fjords or pine trees in black against a background of light blues and pinks which are set over a guilloche and achieve an attractive northern lights effect. More recently Norwegian manufacturers appear to have abandoned the moonstone top in favour of a flat waffle indented top and the thimbles are now decorated with a printed pattern of roses and foliage against a white background.

Germany also has a long-standing reputation for fine enamels and has produced enamel thimbles in quantity. There is an interesting eighteenth-century specimen made of silver with enamel decoration in the Fondazione Artistica Poldi-Pezzoli (Poldi Museum) collection at Milan. From the nineteenth century onwards, various factories produced gold and silver thimbles with a hand-painted design round the base and this type of thimble is still made. Unfortunately the quality of the work has deteriorated progressively. Printed designs have replaced hand-painting particularly where silver is concerned, and since the war the standards have deteriorated further. The silver is more heavily machined, simulated stone tops of glass or plastic are used instead of cornelian, the printed nature of the design has become more obvious and the enamel has a plastic look about it. Nevertheless these thimbles retain some popularity and sell successfully in many countries, thus maintaining Germany's reputation as a traditional exporter of thimbles. The usual decoration consists of posies of roses but modern German enamel thimbles are also produced with printed reproductions of famous monuments in different parts of the world where they are sold as tourist souvenirs. Collectors will know the silver thimbles sold in Holland

25 Norwegian enamel on silver thimbles.
(Private collection)

which are decorated with hand-painted blue enamel Delft-like scenes but they may not be aware that these are imported from Germany.

Good quality enamel thimbles can be found originating from other countries which have not been mentioned, notably France and Italy, and we should not forget Persia (Iran) which also has an established reputation in this respect. The difficulty is that standards of enamelling vary widely. As a general rule the older the work the better it is and finely enamelled thimbles are necessarily among the gems of any collection.

26 Yellow gold ornamented with two garlands of green gold. Inscribed 'Aimée Poumaroux'. French, eighteenth-century. Height 2·8 cm. *(Private collection)*

Gold thimbles

It is impossible to say when gold was first used for making thimbles but there is every reason to believe that by the fourteenth century gold was already competing with silver for the manufacture of thimbles to grace the fingers of queens and princesses. Certainly by the sixteenth century a lady of quality might be expected to possess a gold thimble which would be suitably decorated and possibly surrounded with precious stones. Not many specimens from the sixteenth and seventeenth centuries remain in existence.

During the eighteenth century the use of gold thimbles grew enormously, particularly in France where the gold thimble became something of a status symbol. Under Louis XVI there was a fashion for gold thimbles decorated round the rim with garlands of different coloured golds. In England also gold was increasingly used, often decorated with jewels set close to the rim where the needle would not dislodge the stones. The earliest American gold thimble on record was made by Jacob Hurd (1702-1758) and may be seen in the Yale University Gallery. By the nineteenth century gold thimbles were relatively commonplace. In Europe gold thimbles retained a good deal of individuality but in the United States they were produced largely in the same style as silver thimbles. One noteworthy exception is a plain gold thimble owned by the Museum of Fine Arts, Boston, which was made by Paul Revere (1735-1818) the well-known silversmith and patriot celebrated by Longfellow for his exploit in riding on horseback to warn the inhabitants of Middlesex County of the approach of British troops. This thimble is said to have been one of two and was made with his own hands

27 *Left*. Gold thimble by Jacob Hurd of Boston (1702-1758) marked inside Hurd in oval and engraved Elizabeth Gooch/1714. Engraved with foliated scrolls between two narrow chevron bands; delicately moulded edge. Probably made about 1730-1740. Height 1·7 cm.
(*Yale University Art Gallery*)

28 *Right*. Gold thimble made by Paul Revere about 1805. Height 3·0 cm.
(*Museum of Fine Arts, Boston*)

29 Gold – inscribed E.o.S.
English, possibly seven-
teenth-century. Height 2·0
cm.
(Private collection)

in 1805 for his daughter. By the 1890s gold thimbles had become so
commonplace that they were advertised in the Sears Roebuck catalogue
whilst the well-known firm of Simons Brothers were making to order
gold thimbles set with diamonds at 150 dollars apiece.

Gold thimbles often carry a monogram or cypher and it is tempting to suggest that this could be of help in dating the thimbles concerned. Clearly the style of monograms prevalent during the seventeenth
century is different from that during the eighteenth or nineteenth century but unfortunately it is difficult to take the comparison much further
as styles changed very slowly and several styles might be in use during
the same period depending on the taste or sophistication of the
engraver. Generally speaking the nineteenth century was distinguished

by florid monograms heavily convoluted or with gothic design but even so there are many exceptions which make the dating of thimbles on grounds of the style of lettering an unrewarding pastime. More reliable is the style of armorial bearings and in some cases research may even enable the collector to trace the original owner. What is written here about gold thimbles applies to silver thimbles which were also often engraved with the cypher or monogram of the owner.

In England the use of gold thimbles was at its height during the Victorian era. Such thimbles were manufactured individually with a great variety of decoration but basically the shape remained unchanged throughout the period. The more expensive gold thimbles were set with precious or semi-precious stones; certainly amongst the most beautiful were thimbles decorated with posies of turquoise and worked in several different coloured golds (Plate 8, p. 62). More simply a gold thimble might carry turquoise, pearls or coral inset as a beading round the rim and more simply still the thimble might be worked in plain gold with the goldsmith relying entirely on design to achieve his effect. Some thimbles of this kind are distinctly fussy but others reveal a surprising simplicity and strength of design not normally associated with Victorian taste.

More recently the demand for gold thimbles has declined and few manufacturers continue to make them. Needless to say that gold being costly, silver gilt thimbles were early in evidence. There are two examples of gold plated silver thimbles in the Kunstgewerbemuseum in Berlin which date back to about 1600. Unfortunately the gold on

30 Gold thimbles. Left to right: French art nouveau; Continental with blue enamel and half-pearls; Swedish with fine cornelian stone; French, late nineteenth-century, with multi-coloured gold; United States, dated 1923, with panelled skirting; French traditional design, early nineteenth-century; modern Italian with blue and red enamel. *(Private collection)*

such thimbles tends to wear out fairly quickly and specimens in good condition are relatively rare. Towards the end of the nineteenth century gold-plated silver thimbles were produced in France and specimens will occasionally turn up in the hands of collectors. In accordance with French hallmark regulations, such thimbles carry the boar-head or crab hallmark applicable to silver. A light gilding may also be found in the inside of silver thimbles but this is more in the nature of a finish than of gold-plating as such and is of little significance from the collector's point of view.

Care should be taken in purchasing gold thimbles as there is always the danger of a plain silver thimble being gold-plated and passed off as solid gold. This should not be confused with the silver gilt thimbles mentioned above which are perfectly genuine and easy to distinguish. A genuine silver gilt thimble may be an attractive and worthwhile acquisition but the gold-plated silver thimble intended to pass as gold is a worthless fraud. Collectors should therefore satisfy themselves about what they are buying and when in doubt, seek expert advice. Some gold thimbles are hallmarked which, besides offering a measure of guarantee, can also provide useful information regarding the date and provenance of the thimble.

More will be found about hallmarks in the chapter that discusses silver thimbles but, as always when dealing with thimbles, the more interesting items are often those that are unmarked. Many of the marks are straightforward but one which may occasionally puzzle collectors is a small oval hallmark with the figure of an owl which is sometimes found on some of the older French thimbles. This hallmark *(le hibou)* which was introduced in France in 1893, is applied inter alia to objects which do not bear other means of identification and which are sold through public auctions. The interpretation of hallmarks, however, is a complicated subject and collectors specialising in gold thimbles should consult a good international reference book such as *Les poinçons de garantie internationaux pour l'or et le platine*, 7th edition, published by Tardy of Paris.

Mother-of-pearl thimbles

Plate 3 *(opposite, p. 49, above)*
Meissen porcelain thimble
(marked), about 1740.
*(Museum für Kunst und
Gewerbe, Hamburg)*
(below) English painted en-
amel, South Staffordshire (Bil-
ston), late eighteenth-century.
*(Victoria and Albert Museum,
London)*

Plate 4 *(overleaf, p. 50)*
Eighteenth-century porcelain
thimbles of continental
origin.
(Private collection)

Plate 5 *(overleaf, p. 51,
above left)* Meissen porcelain
thimble (gilt interior)
about 1760.
(Private collection)
(above right) Early thimbles.
Top left, bronze, possibly
Roman. Others are made of
brass, probably sixteenth- to
eighteenth-century.
(Private collection)
(below) On the cushion is a
rare Elizabethan gold thimble
set with alternate rubies and
sapphires, the top with four
rubies in a cross, late sixteenth-century. The remaining thimbles from left to
right are: Derby about 1800;
Bilston enamel; Spode; gold
and tortoise-shell; eighteenth-century Meissen;
Derby (marked) about 1870.
(Dorothy Howell collection)

The use of mother-of-pearl for making thimbles goes back to the Middle Ages or possibly earlier. In Catalonia a text dated 1365 refers to a pedlar bearing ivory thimbles and a thimble of mother-of-pearl: 'Un portador de didaleres de vori, ab una dedalera de nacra'.[30]

Nevertheless thimbles made of mother-of-pearl did not really come into their own until the nineteenth century when mother-of-pearl suddenly became very popular. About 1810, it became the fashion in Paris for small objects in everyday use to be made of mother-of-pearl mounted or bound with gilded bronze or similar material. Such objects were manufactured in great variety including snuff-boxes, cases of various kinds, sewing-boxes and even thimbles. This type of work was conducted by a number of firms situated around the Palais Royal and is now referred to under that name. The fashion soon spread to London, Vienna and elsewhere. Palais Royal thimbles often have one or more bands of gilded metal along the rim or side of the thimble. They are quite distinctive and a charming feature which is sometimes found is a single blue flower, possibly a pansy (Fr. pensée = thought) inserted in the mother-of-pearl, approximately where a crest might be situated if it were a gold thimble. The vogue for mother-of-pearl thimbles was comparatively brief and the majority were manufactured between 1810 and 1815.

Mother-of-pearl is sometimes used in the place of cornelian or other stone and fitted into the tip of a gold thimble where its purpose is to take the wear of the needle.

31 Mother-of-pearl. Two
narrow collars of gilt metal
and a small oval shield decorated with a pansy in blue
enamel. French, about 1810.
Height 2·1 cm.
(Private collection)

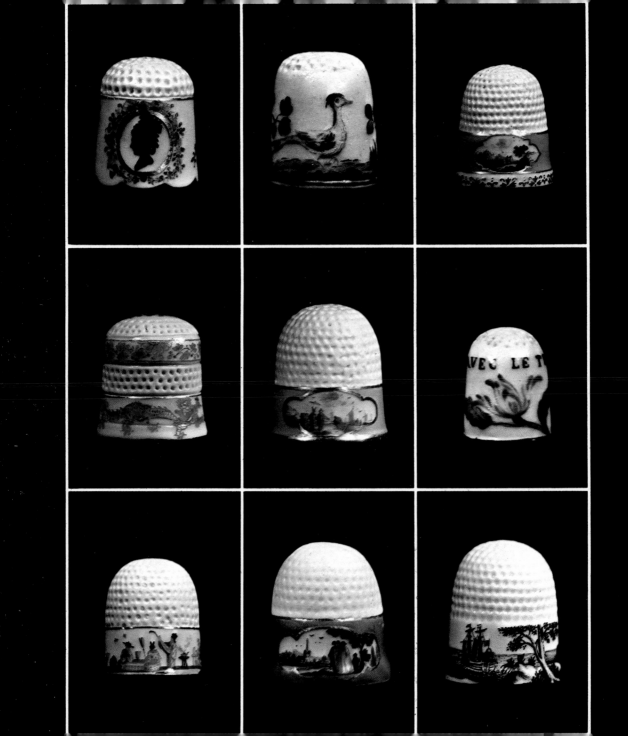

Ivory thimbles

Ivory thimbles have been found among Roman and Gallo-Roman remains and there is little doubt that ivory thimbles were used during the Middle Ages. At least one known example dates from the Renaissance and is carved with the design of a dog coursing after game which was a favourite theme during this period. No doubt others have survived but ivory thimbles are often plain without recognisable motif, dating them is difficult and their shape provides little indication as to their age. Neither can their appearance be of much help since this depends a great deal on the wear and on the conditions under which the thimble was kept. An ivory thimble may be totally discoloured without necessarily being very old and vice versa.

Ivory thimbles may be carved from a single piece of ivory or else in two pieces, the tip being carved separately and screwed into the body. The shape of ivory thimbles tends to vary a great deal, some being long and thin and others surprisingly short and stubby. The rim is occasionally strengthened with a collar of gilt metal.

Ivory thimbles were popular at the end of the eighteenth century or beginning of the nineteenth century when in common with porcelain thimbles they were considered highly suitable for embroidery and lacework, being smooth and pleasant to the touch. One of their principal advantages is that they did not catch on silk threads. In the United States one Charles Shipman of New York advertised ivory thimbles for sale in 1767 but it is not known whether these thimbles were imported or whether they were made locally. Meanwhile in England the fashion for needlework boxes which started about the end of the eighteenth century grew rapidly and by the middle of the nineteenth century quantities of fitted needlework boxes were being imported from abroad. These came chiefly from India which already had a well-established reputation for caskets made of precious woods and from China which was well-known for its lacquer-ware boxes. New designs were developed and the caskets were furnished with sewing tools such as cotton reels, winders, clamps, bodkins, needles and of course a thimble, all made of carved ivory. Work boxes of this kind constituted a very acceptable present but they had the disadvantage that the thimble, not being chosen for size, rarely fitted the finger of the recipient; this probably accounts for the large number of ivory thimbles which have survived in good condition. The fact that these thimbles were made in the Far East also explains why they are so evidently of hand-made artisan manufacture.

At first the trade was largely confined to England but subsequently Indian and Chinese boxes were exported to the Continent and

Plate 6 *(opposite)* Gold thimbles and a gilt metal thimble-holder from a chatelaine; mostly nineteenth-century. *(Private collection)*

32 Ivory – probably oriental, made for European market. Early nineteenth-century. Height 3·0 cm.
(*Private collection*)

33 Ivory thimble with original basket weave holder. Made in China for use of Europeans. About 1830. Height 2·4 cm.
(*Private collection*)

similar thimbles may therefore be found in most Western European countries. Besides the thimbles exported in boxes, Chinese ivory thimbles were also supplied in small individual basket-weave containers which were made specially for the European market. These containers are extremely fine and delicate and few have survived in good condition. As a general rule it is difficult to determine the origin of ivory thimbles with any degree of certainty and as already mentioned they are difficult to date. Unless there is compelling evidence to the contrary, it is fairly safe to attribute ivory thimbles to the nineteenth century as these undoubtedly form the bulk of ivory thimbles in the hands of collectors. Few ivory thimbles have been manufactured during the twentieth century.

A type of ivory thimble will be found which is smooth and without indentations. The origin of such thimbles is obscure but it is believed that they were intended for very fine sewing or embroidery. Ivory thimbles are usually left in their natural colour but specimens occasionally turn up which are tinted or else decorated with a hand-painted floral frieze or other motif round the rim (Plate 8, p. 62).

Ivory thimbles should not be confused with thimbles made of the substance known as vegetable ivory or Corozo nut (see p. 129 below). Vegetable ivory thimbles are scarcer than those made of real ivory and ideally should be collected with a matching thimble case. Thimbles are no longer made of vegetable ivory except in Ecuador where local women use thimbles of vegetable ivory or tagua as it is known in South America. Tagua thimbles are also sold to tourists as gifts and souvenirs.

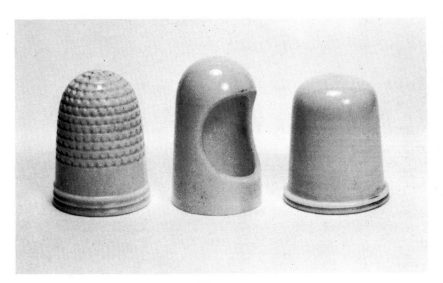

34 Ivory. Left: normal indented thimble. Centre: finger guard. Right: smooth type thimble.
(*Private collection*)

Tortoise-shell thimbles

Tortoise-shell is not really a suitable material for making thimbles although in 1816 John Piercy patented (English patent No. 4077) a process for making thimbles from tortoise-shell, turtle-shell, horn or leather, to be lined, tipped or decorated with iron, steel, silver, gold or other metal. Thimbles made by Piercy's patent are relatively rare and a fine example of tortoise-shell tipped and decorated with gold is illustrated.

35 Gold and tortoise-shell – inscribed Piercy's Patent. English, about 1820. Height 2·7 cm.
(Private collection)

Silver thimbles

Silver is one of the oldest metals known to mankind and has been in use for several thousand years. In its pure form it is very malleable and the addition of some quantity of copper – usually about ten per cent – is necessary to make it hard enough for practical use. Nevertheless even when alloyed with copper, silver remains relatively soft; articles made from it are more vulnerable than is often realised and it is not surprising that really old silver thimbles – and more particularly old silver thimbles in good condition – are rare.

It is not possible to say when silver was first used for thimble-making purposes and although it is probable that silver thimbles were made during the Middle Ages, they were still sufficiently noteworthy during the sixteenth and seventeenth centuries to feature in some wills and inventories of the period. By the eighteenth century silver thimbles had become relatively commonplace. Early thimbles were made in two pieces soldered together much as the latten thimbles mentioned earlier (pp. 9-10). This might be described as the artisan method and it remains the way in which thimbles are made by village silversmiths in remote parts of the world. From the eighteenth century onwards however silver thimbles began to be made by pressing and spinning in a single piece, a method of manufacture which was rapidly adopted among the more industrialised countries and which has remained unchanged to the present time.

The modern silver thimble starts as a plain sheet of silver metal from which is cut a circular disc the size of a large coin. This disc is placed in a powerful press which shapes it into the form of a small cup of approximately the size of the thimble. The cup is softened by heat to release any stresses which may have built up during the pressing process and it is then fitted to a die spigot corresponding to the internal size of the thimble, which is held in a chuck and made to revolve on a lathe. As the cup revolves a series of knurled wheels and other tools are brought to bear with considerable pressure against the sides to impress the indentations, shape any design and trim the edgings. The pattern is engraved by hand and/or machine or it is rolled on, in which case the pattern is cut intaglio on the edge of a narrow steel roller and then pressed into the thimble as it revolves on the lathe. Once the thimble is finished, it is polished both inside and outside after which it is given a final inspection before packaging.

English silver thimbles dating back from before the middle of the eighteenth century, i.e. from before the time when silver thimbles began to be made by pressing and spinning, are rare and there are not many specimens to be found outside the museums. Generally speak-

36 Development of modern
English thimble designs. Left
to right: traditional design, a-
bout 1860 (see fig. 47);
applied fleur de lys band,
Birmingham 1892; decorated
with heart and garland of
gold, Chester 1895; bright
cut engraving of flowers and
leaves by Henry Griffith &
Sons Limited, Birmingham
1902; heavy silver with red,
white and blue beads by
James Swann & Sons
Limited, Birmingham 1936;
modern design by S. J. Rose
& Sons, provisional patent
No. 53211, Birmingham
1965.
(*Private collection*)

37 Design of two cherubs
supporting two hearts
engraved R and N respectively. Possibly seventeenth-century. Height 1·6 cm.
(*Private collection*)

ing silver thimbles from the sixteenth and seventeenth centuries tend to be fairly heavy; they are cylindrical and have a rounded top. They are decorated with patterns which are often quite distinctive: raised chevron or strapwork on a checkered background or all over indentations in the form of small circles. There is a fine example in the London Museum which bears oval medallion portraits of King Charles II and Queen Catherine of Braganza. It is also a feature of these early silver thimbles that many carry a short motto: 'God save the Quene', 'Be not idell', 'In trust bee just', 'A frendes Gifte', 'Feare God and Honour the Kyng' and others. At this time a silver thimble was still an article of value on which silversmiths lavished personal care and attention.

The development of new manufacturing techniques during the eighteenth century brought the silver thimble within the range of mass production. At first the demand for silver thimbles remained uncertain and individual silversmiths continued to produce thimbles as part of their normal activities but after the turn of the century some silversmiths found it worthwhile to specialise and set up thimble-making workshops. Such was the case of Johann Ferdinand Gabler who was born in 1778, the son of a tailor, and who became a silversmith at Shorndorf in Württemberg. Possibly because of his family associations, he gradually came to concentrate on making thimbles and patented a machine for the purpose. His sons built on these beginnings to establish the firm of Gebrüder Gabler G.m.b.H. About 1850 the firm occupied a mill-house as illustrated, but these premises soon became inadequate and the firm prospered to the point that by 1900 Gebrüder Gabler were selling thimbles of gold, silver, brass, steel and other metals on a world-wide scale. Subsequently as demand contracted, the firm diversified into other activities and it finally ceased making thimbles about ten years ago. Similarly George Simons, a Welsh immigrant, established the firm of Simons Brothers and Company in 1839 and set up a thimble factory at Philadelphia. The craft was handed down from father to son and Simons Brothers are the only gold and silver thimble manufacturers still producing thimbles in the United States. In England Henry Griffith set up a thimble factory near Birmingham in 1856 and for almost a hundred years he and his descendants continued making thimbles until 1956 when production was discontinued. For much of this time Henry Griffith and Sons Limited were one of the leading suppliers of silver thimbles in Great Britain and the business prospered so well that, although no longer making thimbles, they remain one of the larger manufacturing goldsmiths and silversmiths in the country. It will be seen from these examples, which are by no means exceptional, that the thimble-making industry grew a great deal during the nineteenth

38 The Gabler family established a thimble factory in this old mill-house at Schorndorf in the Black Forest about 1850. By 1900 Gebrüder Gabler G.m.b.H. thimbles were sold all over the world.

Plate 7 (*opposite*) English porcelain thimbles, mostly nineteenth-century. (*Private collection*)

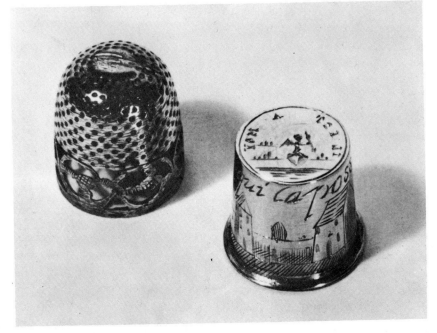

39 Thimble factory 1928.
*(Messrs Henry Griffith and
Sons Limited)*

40 Silver and gold thimble
in two parts: silver left-
hand portion fits over gold
right-hand portion inscribed
'Heureux qui la possède'.
Tip engraved as letter seal
shows cupid and words
'il est a moy'. Late
eighteenth-century.
(Central Museum, Utrecht)

Plate 8 *(opposite, above)*
Hand-painted ivory, early
nineteenth-century.
(British Museum)
(below, left) Enamel on silver-
gilt. Russian, made by Ovcinnikov about 1900.
(Private collection)
(below, right) Gold decorated
with turquoise. English, a-
bout 1860. *(Private collection)*

century. Improved standards of living coupled with a growing population led to a tremendous increase in the demand for silver thimbles which was further stimulated by the Victorian passion for small gifts and souvenirs. This demand lasted until well after the turn of the century when the decline of domestic needlework began to make itself felt. Faced with a falling market, individual manufacturers tried various devices to stimulate demand, e.g. the seaside resort thimbles which Henry Griffith and Sons Limited developed in the 1930s under the brand name 'The Spa' (see p. 112) but these were essentially short-term palliatives and most manufacturers were compelled to discontinue production and to turn their attention elsewhere.

The new machining techniques introduced during the eighteenth century led to a change in the design of thimbles which became lighter and narrower and consequently often appear longer than thimbles of earlier times. Possibly it was easier to work thinner metal or possibly the new techniques enabled silversmiths to use thinner metal with a consequent saving in cost but it was not until the end of the nineteenth century that thimbles reverted to a heavier and squatter appearance. Specimens of silver thimbles dating from much before 1820 are scarce, and they are difficult to distinguish from the thimbles of the early Victorian era, which are found in greater numbers to the point of being relatively commonplace. There are three separate types. First, there is the plain silver thimble which if it dates from the eighteenth century is likely to be made of relatively thin metal with a simple, possibly bright-cut design and no rim around the base. There is a typical Georgian elegance about the design of such thimbles which is in contrast with the Victorian thimble; this tends to be heavier, more ornate and has a rolled or bevelled rim round the base to prevent the edge of the thimble cutting into the finger. The second type is the steel-tipped thimble which, probably because of the relative fragility of silver thimbles, was popular for workaday purposes. It remained popular until the 1880s when it was superseded by the silver thimble with an inner steel core. Such thimbles seldom carried much decoration and the best guide as to age is that like the plain thimble mentioned above, the Georgian steel-tipped thimble is unlikely to have a rim round the base. Lastly, the third type is the filigree thimble which was popular in late Georgian times and which continued to be made until 1830 or thereabouts. The earlier specimens dating from the late eighteenth century are somewhat stubbier than one might expect and have a rounded hemispherical dome with well-spaced and distinctive indentations. By the nineteenth century filigree thimbles had grown longer with the scrolled pattern stretching out to include a shield-shaped or oval panel engraved with the owner's crest or cypher. What must be stressed for

41 English silver filigree thimbles, mostly early nineteenth-century.
(Private collection)

42 English silver filigree toys, early nineteenth-century. Left: thimble, scent bottle and tape measure combined; centre: the same but fitted together; right: thimble, scent bottle and letter seal.
(Private collection)

all three types is that silver thimbles dating back to the eighteenth century are comparatively rare, even thimbles dating back from before the time of Queen Victoria (1837) are scarce, and the bulk of the silver thimbles in the hands of English collectors is likely to be Victorian or later.

Before leaving the Georgian era, it should be mentioned that both plain and filigree thimbles were sometimes combined with some toy or novelty (Plate 2, p. 40). A typical example is that of a plain thimble which forms the cover and screws into a base holding a small cut glass scent bottle with a letter seal underneath. Another is that of a filigree thimble which acts as a cover for a scent bottle and screws into a yard measure. A third screws into a base which holds a pin cushion, the under side of which is engraved to provide a letter seal. There are other combinations and the association of thimbles with letter seals may appear puzzling until it is remembered that skill in letter writing was held in the same esteem as proficiency in needlework; both were regarded as essential ladylike accomplishments and it is not therefore uncommon to find writing and sewing requisites combined. During the eighteenth century ladies were accustomed to use the tip of their thimbles with which to seal a letter and if we are to believe Robert Louis Stevenson, so were sea-faring men, since it will be recalled that the map of Treasure Island was found to be sealed in several places with the Captain's thimble. It is tempting to ascribe these toys and novelties to the eighteenth century but this is not necessarily correct and there are specimens bearing the mark of Joseph Taylor of Birmingham who operated well into the nineteenth century. More typical of the eighteenth century are the German needle-cases with seal and thimble combined. There is a specimen in the Victoria and Albert Museum originating from Augsburg and four fine specimens in the Schweizerisches Landesmuseum, Zurich, which are unmistakable as regards both quality and design.

Yet earlier and going back to the seventeenth century are thimbles with detachable tops. The top of the thimble screws off revealing underneath a small cavity suitable for holding trifles or, as the more sinister-minded will have it, a lethal dose of poison. Seventeenth- and eighteenth-century toys and novelties of this kind are comparatively rare and much sought after.

Coming now to the Victorian era, it is not easy to distinguish early Victorian from mid-Victorian thimbles except that styles became more ornate. The Victorian practice of presenting souvenir thimbles to mark special occasions is also a great help in dating English silver thimbles prior to 1890, when the duty on silver was abolished and silversmiths began to take advantage of the services of the assay office to have their thimbles assayed and marked. As already explained English

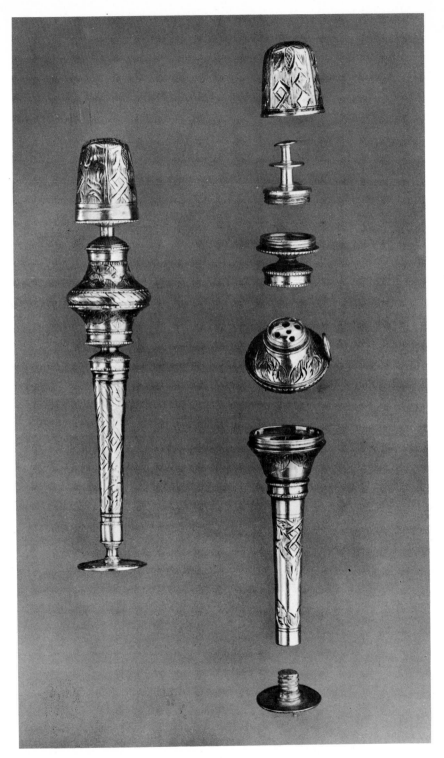

43 Silver sewing case. The thimble covers a small bobbin for thread and the stem serves as a needle case. The foot is adapted to form a letter seal. All the parts screw tightly together. German, late eighteenth-century. Height 11·0 cm.
(The Colonial Williamsburg Foundation)

44 Silver sewing case. German, late eighteenth-century. *(Schweiz. Landesmuseum, Zurich)*

45 Early Victorian thimbles. None of these bear any form of marking whether hallmark or maker's mark. *(Private collection)*

46 English silver thimbles from the first half of the nineteenth century. Left to right: simple bright cut design, inscribed M.P.; filigree inscribed with a crest and the initials G.H.A.; steel top, inscribed Margt Pescod 1819; simple bright cut design, inscribed M.A.J.C.; steel top, unusual pointillé pattern; lightly engraved and inscribed W.W. *(Private collection)*

47 Dating English thimbles. At left, silver thimble inscribed Xmas 1865; centre, silver thimble by George Unite which bears the Queen's Head (rare) and Birmingham mark for 1872; at right, silver thimble with Birmingham hallmark for 1885 and size marking. A common type of thimble during the second half of the nineteenth century. *(Private collection)*

48 More English thimbles. From left to right: applied fleur de lys band, about 1880; the same with different band; stone top hallmarked Chester 1911; blue enamel skirting (nineteenth-century); registered design No. 202312 with inset stones; patriotic thimble from the beginning of the First World War, decorated with coloured enamel and inscribed 'a stitch for the red, white and blue' in blue enamel. *(Private collection)*

49 Silver thimbles from the United States. *(Private collection)*

thimbles carrying a hallmark (as distinct from a maker's mark) or carrying a size number, date with rare exceptions from 1890 or later. Moreover, it seems that once adopted, the practice of marking thimbles became almost universal so that late Victorian thimbles may be dated with accuracy. Thus it is easy to note that during the late Victorian period thimbles once again became stubbier and new designs were introduced which are the forerunners of the twentieth-century English silver thimble as it is known today. Modern English thimbles are quite distinct in style from those in other countries and some of the hand-engraved specimens produced at the turn of the century are particularly fine and would grace any collection.

A danger of mass-producing thimbles is that it is possible to cut down costs by introducing manufacturing techniques which tend to produce a dull and lifeless article. Modern continental thimbles have been particularly affected, for instance, by heavily machined indentations which, 'while cheaper to apply, look uninteresting. It is much to the credit of English manufacturers that they resisted this temptation and thereby have given English thimbles a very distinct style of their own. It is easy to be deceived, for instance, by the floral patterns which take the place of indentations on some of the English thimbles produced in the early 1900s. The very regularity and exactness of the pattern suggests that they were impressed mechanically, but in fact the reason why they are so bright and attractive is that the design was not rolled on but was struck with a cutting tool. Moreover to achieve the necessary degree of sharpness the tools were built up of individual components so that in the case of a flowered pattern it could almost be said that each petal was struck separately. Similar considerations apply to other designs and English silversmiths have produced some of the finest machined silver thimbles to be found anywhere.

The introduction of mass production techniques for silver thimbles in the United States appears to have taken place at about the same time as it did in Europe but with this difference that from the start the American designs were more functional. In Europe, and more particularly in Great Britain, a wide range of thimbles were produced in many different shapes and sizes but American manufacturers tended to restrict themselves more to a few well-established patterns. Several major thimble manufacturers emerged during the nineteenth century – at one time there were no less than six firms manufacturing thimbles in the United States, including the Ketchem and McDougall partnership of Brooklyn, New York. Ketchem and McDougall were among the leading manufacturers until 1932 when they discontinued the manufacture of thimbles. Their trade mark (K & McD) may be found stamped at the apex of many American thimbles. Another trade mark which is very often found is that of Simons Brothers of Philadelphia whose trade mark is a large gothic 'S' in a shield. Other marks which may be found are those of A. T. Gunner Manufacturing Co., Attleboro, Mass. (a letter 'G' in a five-pointed star) and of Thomas S. Brogan of New York, N.Y. (a five-pointed star).

Another feature of American thimbles is that they are usually stamped clearly on the side with a size number. Strange as it may seem, size numbers were not introduced on English thimbles before about 1880 and in Europe to this day there are still manufacturers who do not use size numbers. The style of the size numbers on American thimbles is quite distinctive. The numbers are smaller, neater and more clearly impressed than in Europe and they are a useful help in distinguishing American thimbles from their European counterparts. Any collector specialising in American thimbles is well-advised to consult Miss Lundquist's book on the subject (see Bibliography, p. 146) where he will find that a great number are illustrated.

Turning now to the thimbles of other countries, it is also the case that the older and often more interesting silver thimbles are largely unmarked. Nevertheless there is a great deal of information to be derived from a proper study of hallmarks which for present purposes may be defined as authenticating marks struck after testing to guarantee the standard of quality. The term has also come to include the maker's mark. Most countries have a system of hallmarking silver which sometimes also includes a date code and helps to date the piece in question with accuracy. Unfortunately, thimbles are so small that they were often exempt either because the duty payable was too small to justify marking or else because of the danger of damaging the design. Nevertheless when a thimble is hallmarked it is a help towards determining its provenance and in some cases its date of manufacture. It should be remembered however that just because a thimble bears one country's hallmark, it does not necessarily follow that it was produced there and it may well have been imported. Some countries have special hallmarks to denote imported silver but the rules vary. The interpretation of hallmarks is a specialised and complicated subject and it is not possible to give more than a few hints to help collectors place some of the more frequently occurring items:

Austro-Hungary

In earlier days the standard unit of purity in central Europe was the loth which was equal to ·0625 so that 13 löthige was ·8125 and 12 löthige ·750. The loth was discontinued about 1860 so that thimbles bearing a hallmark showing the numbers 12 or 13 are likey to date from the eighteenth or nineteenth century and to emanate from central Europe.

England

The Lion Passant, sometimes called the sterling mark, denotes that the silver is 92·5 per cent pure. Providing the hallmarks are legible the British system of hallmarking enables the collector to determine the exact year of manufacture. English thimbles normally carry the Birmingham mark (anchor) or Chester (dagger between three wheat sheaves) and only occasionally the Sheffield or London mark. English thimbles dating from before 1890 are mostly unmarked.

France

French hallmark regulations are complicated but as a general rule French thimbles manufactured since 1838 should carry firstly a maker's mark in a diamond-shaped outline and secondly a boar's head (Paris) or a crab (Provinces) either at the rim or in that portion of the thimble between the border and the indentations. Imported thimbles or those of doubtful origin may also be found with a hallmark in the shape of a swan.

50 French silver thimbles, nineteenth-century. *(Private collection)*

Germany

Since 1888 silver should bear the registered mark of the maker, the silver content, and if over ·800 a hallmark consisting of a crown and moon. Modern German thimbles normally carry a figure denoting the silver content and nothing more.

Italy

Since 1935 Italian silver bears the registered number of the maker together with the title, i.e. ·800 or ·925. It would appear that silversmiths in Italy were fairly free from any regulations designed to impose a standard until 1935.

Netherlands

A minute letter 'Z' will sometimes be found impressed on the outside of modern thimbles at the apex. This denotes an imported thimble (usually from Germany), the code being ZI for ·925, ZII for ·835 and Z only for ·800. Older thimbles may be hallmarked.

Norway

Since 1891 the hallmark shows the purity of the silver which is a minimum of ·830 and is followed by the letter 'S'. There is also a title of ·925S which will be found on enamel thimbles. These marks will normally be found inside the thimble at the apex.

Portugal

Portuguese thimbles normally carry two marks, one a maker's mark and the other the official hallmark which from 1866 to 1938 has been an eagle's head or a boar's head with a Roman I denoting a purity of ·916 or a Roman II denoting a purity of ·833. The outline of the mark varies depending on whether it was struck in Lisbon, Oporto or elsewhere. Since 1938 the official hallmark has been the head of a cockerel with the title, whether ·916 or ·833 incorporated underneath.

Russia

Until 1925 the unit of purity was the Solothnik representing 1/96th of a Russian pound. Pure silver was therefore 96 Solothniks. The most common title is 84 Solothniks (·875) so that thimbles bearing a hallmark showing the number 84 (or since 1927 the number 875) are likely to come from Russia.

Sweden

The official state hallmark since 1912 consists of two marks, the first showing the three Swedish crowns and the second the letter 'S'. A date code may also be found.

United States

American thimbles often carry the mark of the maker or distributor stamped inside the thimble at the apex. Since the 1860s American thimbles carry the mention 'sterling' or 'sterling silver' which denotes a purity of ·925.

Deciphering hallmarks calls for considerable experience and reference books such as the one published by Tardy or more specialised works such as Jackson's are essential. [31] In many cases however, hallmarks are superfluous or merely serve to confirm what is otherwise obvious to an experienced collector. A collector of English thimbles should have no difficulty in recognising an English thimble without looking at the hallmark and with practice should even be able to make a guess at the hallmark with a fair degree of accuracy. Similarly the collector will soon come to recognise the somewhat longer and slimmer look of French thimbles. There is a wide range of French thimbles with an applied skirting in silver or silvergilt which is quite unmistakable, and in a different style no one who has ever seen a French thimble with a design based on one of La Fontaine's fables such as 'Le Corbeau et le Renard', 'Le Loup et la Cigogne' or 'Le Lièvre et la Tortue', can ever mistake this type again irrespective of whether it carries a hallmark or not. Where the hallmark may be useful is in the process of acquiring the necessary knowledge or as a means of confirming the collector's judgment.

The style of American thimbles is equally distinctive and an experienced collector should be able to recognise many American thimbles at a glance and in some cases may even be able to tell the name of the maker without troubling to look for the maker's mark. American silversmiths evolved their own style of thimble which tends to be less ornate and more conservative than its counterparts in Europe. The early introduction of mass-production methods may have influenced the design but the finish is good and ornamental scrollwork, beading and

51 Silver – traditional French design illustrating La Fontaine fables. More rarely this style of thimble may be found in gold.
(Private collection)

52 Silver – in the shape of a finger nail. Patent No. 19157. London 1905. Height 2·2 cm. (*Private collection*)

channelling is almost invariably of a high standard. The general squatness of American silver thimbles may have been of some assistance by requiring less stretch of the metal and allowing greater thickness. Possibly the more noteworthy are the nineteenth-century silver thimbles with stylised panoramic views – coast scenes with harbours, lighthouses and sailing boats, town scenes with buildings, rivers and bridges, and country scenes with farm houses, trees and mountains. There is a pleasing simplicity about many of the designs and this type of thimble is quite unmistakably American.

The dating of American thimbles presents the usual difficulties though the trade-marks can often be helpful. The practice of marking thimbles with the name of the manufacturer or merchant is a useful clue and so is the word 'sterling' denoting the standard of gold or silver purity. American gold and silver thimbles did not normally carry a mark until the 1860s when the word 'sterling' was introduced to show 92·5 per cent fine metal content. There are no hallmarks in the United States and the 'sterling' mark thus merely provides an indication of the country of origin and suggests that the article in question is less than a hundred years old.

Another type of marking which is sometimes found on American or British thimbles is a patent date or number or the number of a registered design. Thimbles incorporating special features or developments might be the subject of a patent in which case the date of the patent is shown on American thimbles while the patent number under which the invention is registered appears on British thimbles. A typical example is illustrated showing a thimble shaped like the tip of a finger complete with an indentation on one side to simulate a nail. It is doubtful whether a thimble made to look like a finger nail is particularly convenient for sewing but the idea is an old one and Meissen is reputed to have made a thimble of this type in unglazed porcelain. Moreover it was obviously saleable because the same shape may be found not only in silver but also in cupro-nickel and in plastic. According to Elizabeth Aldridge it was advertised as 'The only thimble which has obtained a certificate for Hygienic Merit. Perfect fitting. Prices: white metal $9\frac{3}{4}$d each, plain silver $1/11\frac{1}{2}$d each. Chased $2/6\frac{1}{2}$d each. Fancy $2/9\frac{1}{2}$d each in box'.[32] This was patented (British patent No. 19157) and, as such, is different from the thimble in the shape of a Scottish thistle which was the subject of a registered design (Rd. No. 222445) – see illustration. Registered numbers arise from the Patents Design and Trade Marks Act of 1883 under which designers were able to register and secure protection for unusual designs as distinct from actual inventions. The date of registration may be estimated from the fact that the numbers are consecutive, starting in 1883, and had reached 600,000 by about 1910. Date of registration would not of course necessarily be the same as the date of manufacture and the hallmark remains the best indication.

Among the more distinctive silver thimbles are those from India which are certainly among the most attractive (Plate 2, p. 40). Indian thimbles are almost invariably hand-made and, whilst Indian artisan silversmiths have been known to produce plain and insignificant items, others, notably from the Cutch area which is noted for its silverwork, are gloriously elaborate. One of the thimbles in the illustration was catalogued by a leading London auction room as English Georgian silver and this type of thimble has also been referred to as early eighteenth-century but this is mistaken. Not only is the style wrong but so is the method of construction, since a Georgian thimble would in all likelihood be turned on a lathe. At the end of the last century the Army and Navy stores were offering for sale thimbles made of Indian silver and it is possible that Indian silver thimbles were imported into England about this time or that they were brought back from India as souvenirs, but either way such thimbles are relatively commonplace and can still be found in India in fair quantities.

Many interesting hand-worked thimbles have been produced in the Near East and in the Far East, but few of these are marked and the collector must be guided by his own judgment. Here it is relevant to mention a device which is sometimes found consisting of a silver thimble attached to a ring by a small chain. The ring is slipped on the finger and when the thimble is not in use it is allowed to hang by the chain until required. No doubt this saved a good deal of thimble hunting and specimens have been noted from Southern Russia, Turkestan and Iran, suggesting that it is mainly a Near Eastern development.

53 Silver – in the shape of a Scottish thistle. Registered design No. 222445. Birmingham 1893. Height 2·6 cm. *(Private collection)*

54 Silver – decorated with flowers and foliage. Indian, late nineteenth-century. Height 2·4 cm. *(Private collection)*

55 Ring and chain. At left, thimble from Turkestan, ring is decorated with cornelian, early twentieth-century. At right, modern silver-gilt Russian thimble decorated with black and blue enamel. *(Private collection)*

56 Russian niello decorated silver thimble, late nineteenth-century. Height 2·2 cm.
(Private collection)

57 Silver thimbles from the Near East. Left to right: primitive niello type decoration round base; engraved with floral design, Persia; niello birds and flowers; blue enamel, Persia; plain design with eye for ring and chain; Egypt, nineteenth-century.
(Private collection)

Another type of silver thimble which is quite distinctive is that decorated with niello work. Niello is a method of ornamenting silver by engraving the surface and filling up the lines with a black composition to give clearness and effect to the design. The Russian town of Tula was a well-known manufacturing centre for niello decorated silver ware in Czarist time, and niello decorated thimbles which were sold as tourist souvenirs in the Caucasus will occasionally be found. Russian silver is normally hallmarked but the marks are difficult to read. Niello decorated thimbles also originate from the Middle East. These have smooth sides and are decorated with views of the Nile or associated designs and were sold to tourists before the war. The exact country of manufacture is uncertain but could be Iran.

It would not be possible to comment individually on all the different types of silver thimbles, only some of which are referred to in these pages. Some fine silver thimbles were made in Germany and are still made there and exported to many parts of the world. Greece makes very distinctive silver thimbles and so does Mexico whose thimbles have found their way to many collections. Spain and Portugal have special styles of thimbles and so has Italy where there is a long tradition of thimble-making. But besides all these, there remain many interesting thimbles which are difficult to place and which are probably best described as 'continental'. Thimble manufacturing has always been an important activity in Central Europe, but in the present state of knowledge it is not always possible to determine where a thimble comes from and the 'continental' designation to cover European thimbles of unknown origin is highly convenient.

Finally, it is as well to remember that silver thimbles are relatively common and that, whilst there are many fine specimens, there are also a great many which are totally devoid of interest. An irritating habit of dealers who do not know about thimbles is to comment that a thimble they have for sale is made of 'real' silver and to infer thereby that silver being a precious metal the thimble is a good one. Nothing could be further from the truth. In the first place the value of the silver in a thimble is negligible – in 1928 Woolworth were selling silver thimbles at sixpence each, equivalent to about $12\frac{1}{2}$ cents at the time – and, silver being one of the most common materials for thimble making, it follows that many silver thimbles are of little interest. What is much more important and distinguishes a good silver thimble from a bad one is age, condition, the nature of the decorations and above all the quality of workmanship. Many silver thimbles are quite magnificent – such as would grace any collection – but the fact that a thimble is made of silver is in itself of no consequence and the collector will do well to disregard it.

58 Three silver thimbles of unknown origin – possibly late nineteenth-century Dutch.
(*Private collection*)

Bone thimbles

Although thimbles made of bone have been produced in large numbers over the centuries and, as we saw earlier, bone thimbles have been found among Gallo-Roman remains, nevertheless genuine bone thimbles are comparatively rare. Such specimens as do turn up are also difficult to date. In England it is reported that bone thimbles were made by French prisoners-of-war between 1756 and 1815[33] but this is unconfirmed. More often than not thimbles said to be made of bone are found to be made of ivory, vegetable ivory, or early plastic-type substances such as celluloid or casein. It is not always easy to distinguish between bone and ivory but generally bone contains minute tubes so that where the surface cuts across the grain the tubes get filled with dirt and they show as small black specks. Ivory on the other hand is smoother and shows silky stripes of slightly varying colours.

Bone thimbles will occasionally be found which have a metal waffle-indented cap fitted into the tip to take the wear of the needle and which are decorated with a design, e.g. the head of a reindeer burnt round the sides with a red hot needle. These originate from Lapland.

59 Bone thimbles. At left, nineteenth-century English; centre, origin unknown; at right, from Lapland with metal top and design of a reindeer.
(Private collection)

Horn thimbles

Horn is not a suitable material for thimble-making as it tends to be too soft and it splits rather easily. Nevertheless it is sometimes used where nothing better is available and the accompanying illustration shows an example of a ring-type thimble made of buffalo horn and originating from an outlying village in the Indian State of Bihar.

A type of horn thimble will be found which is smooth and without indentations. This dates from the nineteenth century and it is unclear whether such items were designed as thimbles or whether they were in fact finger guards.

60 Horn ring-type thimble. Indian, nineteenth-century. Height 2·1 cm. *(Private collection)*

Leather thimbles

There is every reason to think that until about the fourteenth century most thimbles were made of leather although, regrettably, these early thimbles have not survived. Indeed we cannot even be sure what these early thimbles looked like. Some would have it that they consisted of a band of leather sewn in a ring with a stitched-on cap, and an example used in County Cork up to about the year 1820 is described in the records of the British Archeological Association. This, however, may have been a later development. As we have seen, our forebears tended to sew with the side of the finger and therefore it is more likely that early leather thimbles were constructed on the lines of the two thimbles illustrated on page 8. These are, in fact, relatively modern but they were obtained from outlying villages in Outer Mongolia and since the Mongols, in common with most other Far Eastern people, tend to sew with the side of the finger, it is not unreasonable to think that they may be very similar to the thimbles which were used in Europe before the leather fingerling gave way to the metal thimmel.

More sophisticated ring-type thimbles made of leather are in everyday use in Japan. Leather thimbles are also used in Korea. A modern leather thimble of unknown origin and designed to be used sideways since it has a hole at the top is shown in the illustration.

An interesting item which arose in London at a sale of antiques and bygones, was a ring-type leather thimble attached to a leather bracelet. The thimble consisted essentially of a band of leather to fit round the thumb and the attachment was intended to keep the thimble hanging close at hand when not in use. In all probability this was a home-made article designed by an artisan such as a leather worker or sail-maker accustomed to doing a good deal of heavy stitching. The item was said to be Elizabethan but no great reliance can be placed on this as leather is difficult to date with any accuracy.

61 Leather – unknown origin.
Height 2·8 cm.
(*Private collection*)

Glass thimbles

Glass has occasionally been used for the manufacture of thimbles but authentic specimens are rare. The British Museum possesses a fine example made of plain cut glass decorated with cross hatchings and there is another in the collection of the Colonial Williamsburg Foundation in the United States which has a crenellated rim. There are also a few known examples in private collections. The origin of these thimbles is obscure and the best that can be said is that they probably date back from the early part of the nineteenth century. Thimbles of opaline glass are also known dating from the late nineteenth or early twentieth century. Otherwise thimbles are reported to have been made of Venetian and Bohemian glass but this remains unverified.

Certain items of Nailsea glass are sometimes claimed to be thimbles but these are delicate, they have a smooth top without indentations and it is unlikely that they were made for the purpose. More recently some rudimentary glass thimbles have appeared for sale but these are modern items unsuitable for sewing and best disregarded.

62 Cut glass thimble decorated with cross-hatchings. Probably nineteenth-century. Height 2·6 cm.
(*Private collection*)

Stone thimbles

Thimbles are occasionally made of stone, notably jade, which because of its extreme hardness and close texture, is not ill-suited for the purpose. Jade thimbles, as might be expected, originate from China. Thimbles have also been made of onyx which is a variety of chalcedony with flat-sided colour bands.

More often, silver, gold or even wooden thimbles are tipped with a hard stone whose purpose is to take the wear of the needle. Probably the most commonly used is cornelian which is a reddish or reddish-brown variety of chalcedony. Other stones which may also be found include amethyst, a purple or bluish-violet variety of quartz; a-gate, layers of quartz of different tints; moss agate, a variety of chalcedony with inclusions resembling moss; bloodstone, a dark green variety

63 Silver gilt – set with amethyst top and an amethyst skirting. Italian, about 1900. Height 2·2 cm.
(*Private collection*)

of chalcedony variegated with jasper and in the case of Norwegian thimbles, moonstone which is a variety of feldspar. There are many others and thimbles with stone tops are an interesting and colourful addition to a collection.

It is not known where or when the practice of fitting thimbles with stone tops was first introduced but there is good reason to believe that it originated in northern Europe. Certainly by the end of the eighteenth century silver and gold thimbles fitted with cornelian tops were in use in Scandinavia. Several specimens dating from the early nineteenth century may be seen at the Halwylska Palatzet museum near Stockholm and there is also a Swedish gold thimble tipped with cornelian in the Berlin Kunstgewerbemuseum which was made by Johann Daniel Blomsterwall (181?/1841) and is therefore of the same period. Thimbles with stone tops were also produced in Germany and the United Kingdom but in the case of the latter, the stone instead of resting on a base of metal is merely mounted in a recess and gripped round the edge so that the stone appears translucent if the thimble is held up to the light. Such thimbles are sometimes referred to as 'Scottish' thimbles though there would appear to be little evidence linking them with Scotland. On the contrary one popular model in vogue shortly after the turn of the century was ringed with a shamrock and harp design and had a green stone top said to be made from Connemara

64 Stone tops. Left to right: Moss agate (green), silver, continental; cornelian (red), silver, German; moonstone (white), gold, Northern Europe, inscribed 1893; amethyst (violet) silver, continental; agate (black and white stripes), silver, English. Most of these date from the end of the nineteenth century or thereabouts.
(Private collection)

marble. But whether 'Scottish' or 'Irish', the manufacture of this type of thimble was concentrated in the hands of the Birmingham silversmiths who produced thimbles with stone tops in large quantities. The stones were bought ready cut and with the necessary indentations from a manufacturing silversmith's supplier and it remained for the thimble manufacturer to fit each thimble with a stone and to ensure that the stone was fixed securely into position.

More recently the use of stone tops for thimbles has been discontinued and in their place thimble manufacturers have come to use simulated stones made of plastic. These have been used to cap silver, brass and aluminium thimbles. Simulated stone tops tend to give a comparatively cheap effect to thimbles and they are best avoided.

65 Silver – set with agate top. English, Birmingham 1896. Height 2·1 cm. The thimble stands among loose hardstone tops as used by thimble makers.
(*Private collection*)

Wooden thimbles

Wood has never been popular for making thimbles because it tends to be soft and splits easily. Nevertheless the vogue for small articles made of wood in England in the early nineteenth century led to the manufacture of wooden thimbles, sometimes with matching cases. Mulberry wood and boxwood were used among others. Wooden thimbles are difficult to date but some early Tunbridge thimbles which have circular rings instead of indentations and several red painted lines round the base are unmistakable. There are also thimbles made of the later Tunbridge stickware. Many of these thimbles were beautifully turned but wooden thimbles never achieved the same advantages as metal thimbles and consequently were never produced in any quantity. During the latter part of the nineteenth century thimbles made of ebony were

66 Wood – base decorated with two red bands and one blue band; English, early Tunbridge, about 1800. Height 2·5 cm.
(Private collection)

67 Wooden thimble with cornelian stone top. Probably German.
(Private collection)

recommended for embroidery and these became known by the name of Nuns' thimbles.

On the Continent, thimbles were produced in France at the beginning of the nineteenth century made of sandalwood and decorated round the rim with a cut steel border and nails. The odour of sandalwood thimbles when kept in work baskets was reputed to keep away moths. Wooden thimbles were also produced in large quantities in Germany and Austria where they were sold as souvenirs for tourists. Some of these were made of boxwood. Occasionally the wood is capped with cornelian or other stone for added strength. More workmanlike are the Irish bog oak thimbles which are hard and resistant. Bog oak is semi-petrified wood excavated from the Irish bogs; it is black and resembles ebony.

In the Far East villagers have been known to use bamboo which when carefully selected for size can be made into an efficient thimble. Also in India ring-type thimbles are hand-carved from sandalwood for sale to collectors.

In the United States souvenir thimbles made from orange wood are known from California. An American artisan, Conan Fisher, is currently making thimbles in various woods for sale to collectors.

Collectors may sometimes come across large white-painted wooden thimbles or similar thimbles made of white plastic. These are not intended for sewing but are stage properties designed for the purpose of conjuring tricks by professional magicians.

68 Wooden thimbles. Left to right: Child's thimble and case, early nineteenth-century; nineteenth-century, of unknown origin; Irish bog oak inscribed 'BRAY'; ebony, so-called nun's thimble, nineteenth-century; English, nineteenth-century. *(Private collection)*

Fabric thimbles

Thimbles made of textile fabric handstitched over a padded cardboard framework are used in Japan and other Far Eastern countries. These are usually in bright colours and may include an embroidered motif.

Contemporary brass thimbles surrounded with a band of petit point (or sometimes hand embroidery) are made in Austria and Hungary.

69 Fabric thimbles from Korea.
(Private collection)

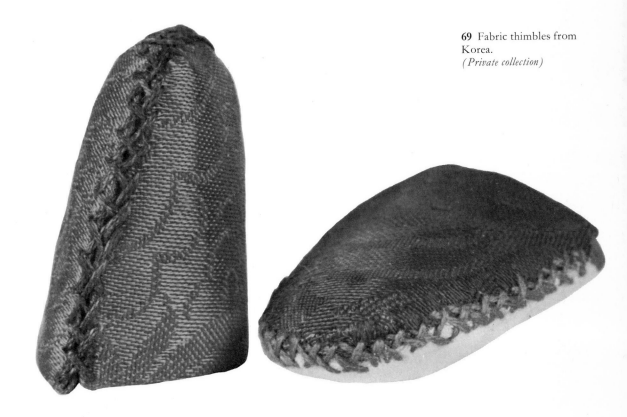

Brass thimbles

The earliest thimbles which have survived were made of bronze i.e. an alloy of copper and tin which was already in widespread use by the time of the Romans. Molten bronze being relatively easy to cast into moulds, bronze thimbles were normally made by this process.

By the Middle Ages latten had largely replaced bronze in the making of thimbles. Latten is an alloy of copper and zinc very similar to brass but with the zinc derived from calamine, a zinc ore which was mostly mined in Flanders. The alloy was cast into ingots and was flattened into sheets by means of batteries of water-driven hammers. Until about the middle of the sixteenth century latten or battery metal as it was also known, was imported into England from the Continent. Subsequently the use of calamine was abandoned in favour of a purer form of zinc, and latten came to be known as brass or 'yellow metal', another name used at the time. The word brass is in fact a generic term used to cover a wide range of alloys composed of copper and zinc in varying proportions. A high proportion of copper yields a reddish coloured brass whereas a higher proportion of zinc makes for a yellower tone – a typical brass alloy being composed of approximately 70 per cent copper and 30 per cent zinc.

English medieval thimbles and the later Tudor thimbles made of brass are by no means uncommon but dating them is extremely difficult and at best is largely an exercise in guess work. There are few evolutionary pointers which can be used as guides and moreover the changes in sewing habits consequent on the introduction of more sophisticated needles, the disappearance of the leather fingerling, the different uses for which thimbles were intended making for variations in size, thickness and coarseness of indentations, and finally the international trade in thimbles even during early times, make it impossible to establish a pattern. Nevertheless the following notes may be of interest:

Size and weight

Earlier thimbles are heavier, thicker and of a size designed for wearing on a man's thumb. Later thimbles are lighter, thinner and more likely to be of a size designed for wearing on a lady's finger.

Shape

Earlier thimbles tend to be round and squat. Later thimbles may be thinner and longer.

Construction

Earlier thimbles tend to be made from a single piece of metal. Later thimbles may be made of two pieces with the sides formed from a strip of metal brazed at the joint, and the cap fitted separately on top. By the end of the seventeenth century, however, brass thimble manufacturers had reverted to single piece construction.

Indentations

Earlier thimbles have hand-punched indentations in no set pattern. Then follow hand-punched indentations set in an orderly pattern, e.g. vertical lines or more commonly a spiral beginning at the open end and continuing up into the crown. There is sometimes a stamped maker's mark preceding the first indentation at the commencement of the spiral. Then follow mechanically impressed indentations set in a spiral beginning at the open end and continuing up into the crown. These may also have a stamped maker's mark. Later thimbles, i.e. from about the end of the seventeenth century, have the indentations applied mechanically round the sides in a wide strip as at the present time. The crown is stamped or indented separately. Modern thimbles have the indentations applied together to both the sides and the crown.

70 Brass – in three sizes corresponding to girls', maids' and women's fittings. Late eighteenth-century. *(Private collection)*

Crown

Early thimbles usually have a bare crown and if the thimble is indented with a spiral, this terminates before reaching the centre. A thimble with a bare crown is likely to date from before 1650.

Rim and decoration

The earliest thimbles have no rim or decoration. Later thimbles may have no rim but a single incised or lightly hand-punched line. Still later thimbles have the open end rolled outwards or have a separate band attached round the outside. Such thimbles are also likely to be decorated.

It cannot be stressed too strongly, however, that the above is merely a guide to enable the collector to know what features to look for. In practice the only way to date an old brass thimble with any accuracy is to relate it to other objects with which it may have been found; in this connection a recent find of half-a-dozen thimbles from dated (medieval) archeological levels at Baynard's Castle is of major interest and in due course may throw welcome light on the subject.

Brass thimbles have of course been manufactured in enormous quantities and by the end of the seventeenth century were already commonplace. 'Why didst thou not bring thy thimble? Hast thou ne'er a brass thimble clinking in thy pocket ...' says Lady Wishefort sarcastically to her maid.[34] As we have seen, by this time John Lofting's factory in Islington (1695) was capable of casting an average of 140 gross per week and although it is unlikely that the factory ever operated at full capacity, nevertheless the population of England at the time was about five million which suggests that there was a market for several hundred thousand thimbles per annum. It is surprising that not more of these thimbles have survived. Probably the best collection is that of the London Museum which has a good selection in reserve including an interesting item of some forty thimbles which were discovered at the bottom of a well in St. Martin's-le-Grand on the outskirts of the City of London. What the thimbles were doing down a well can only be a matter of conjecture but close examination suggests that they were made by the same method employed by John Lofting and it is possible therefore that they originated in the first place from nearby Islington.

It is probable that in the United States small artisan manufacturers were producing thimbles during the seventeenth century, but in all likelihood large-scale production did not really get under way before 1700, i.e. about the same time that Lofting imported Dutch techniques into England. Thimbles are mentioned in an American inventory dated 1711, 'Three dozen and one of thimbles at 2d ye thimble'

(Springfield Rec. II 42). These were obviously base metal and almost certainly brass but unfortunately it is impossible to know whether they were locally made or imported.

During the nineteenth century brass thimbles were produced in enormous quantities and from about 1850 onwards inventors turned their attention towards improving thimbles and devising gadgets to go with them. In Britain Charles Marsden, self-styled inventor and manufacturer, patented a ventilated thimble in 1851, described as a thimble with an inner casing between which and the outer casing a space was provided for the escape of perspiration. He exhibited his patent ventilated thimbles together with elastic finger guards with a silver shield and sundry other items at the Great International Exhibition that year. This was followed in 1857 by C. Iles – no doubt on behalf of the well known English manufacturers of the same name – who patented the lining of thimbles with a non-metallic product. Brass thimbles in particular are hard on the finger and the coating of the inside of the thimble with some suitable compound or paintstuff was a noteworthy advance which found commercial application. Then came other inventions such as Taylor's non-slip patent (which however may not have been patented). This was a brass thimble with a ridge round the top of the thimble thus preventing the head of the needle from slipping down the sides. There were also British patents covering thimbles with thread cutting and needle threading attachments. In 1905 A. Nielson patented a needle-threader consisting of a conical or funnel-shaped hole

71 Brass thimbles with gadgets. Left to right: hexagonal shaped with needle-threading attachment (Reg. No. 711917); threader thimble; Taylor's non-slip patent; Pursall's patent peep-show thimble; thimble with threading device; another threading device.
(Private collection)

which was used to guide the thread through the eye of a needle inserted in another hole situated perpendicularly to it. In 1906 E. Dassler and A. Schneider patented a thimble with an internal spring to grip the finger. In 1907 C. S. Biggon and H. W. Gallic patented a thimble combined with a thread-cutter mounted in a slide recessed in the head of the thimble. In 1908 C. E. Iles – presumably a descendant of the C. Iles who took out a patent in 1857 – took out three patents: one covering the lining of thimbles with sheet celluloid or similar flexible material; another in respect of a ventilated thimble allowing air to circulate; and a third concerning a method of fixing a non-metallic lining to a metal thimble. Even the first World War did not dampen the enthusiasm of inventors who continued to patent improvements – mostly thread cutting devices – until the late twenties when the flow of inventions finally dried up and the inventors presumably turned their attention elsewhere.

Not all the inventions reached the stage of commercial production, but nevertheless about the turn of the century travelling salesmen were going round towns, villages and country fairs selling brass thimbles with various attachments or improvements which they sought to promote much as kitchen gadgets are now promoted in the market place. These attachments were usually designed to thread the needle or to provide a means of cutting thread without resorting to scissors, or both. One such thimble patented in the United States had a moveable needle threader and razor at the side to cut thread and it is not difficult to imagine the sales patter which was used to persuade the public of the absolute necessity of owning such novelties. It seems that like so many gadgets which look attractive in the hands of a skilled salesmen, they proved of little practical value in the home. Few examples have survived and even fewer are still in use. A more modern idea is that of the contemporary German cupro-nickel thimble which has a small magnet built in the tip. In theory this is used to pick up pins but in practice it is open to question whether many women would want to use a thimble for this purpose or whether a full size magnet might not prove more efficient.

Possibly even more impractical was a British patent taken out by W. Pursall in 1880 for a novelty consisting of a thimble with a peep-show built into the tip. Brass thimbles of this kind showing the photograph of a popular tourist resort were sold as souvenirs and specimens exist with views of Dolgelly, Ipswich and the Forth Bridge. Needless to say, a thimble so equipped is largely useless because the peep-hole gets in the way of the needle and it would seem that the demand was limited because peep-show thimbles are relatively scarce.

Brass thimbles being intended for workaday purposes, they are normally plainer and less ornate than thimbles made of more precious metals but it would be a mistake to think that all brass thimbles are necessarily dull and unattractive. Many are admittedly of little interest to the collector but there are some brass thimbles which are excellently designed and some, particularly among the English Victorian thimbles, which compare favourably with their silver counterparts. Some brass thimbles are impressive because of their robustness such as, for instance, 'Her Majesty' brass thimbles. These probably date from about 1830 when shortly after William IV came to the throne Queen Adelaide announced her intention to ban French fashions from the court. The purpose of this 'Buy British' campaign' was to counteract the delayed post-war depression which hit the British textile and fashion trades during the years 1826-30. Side branches of the drapery and haberdashery trade found it worthwhile to jump on the bandwaggon and it is probable that 'Her Majesty' thimbles were designed for the purpose. However this could be mistaken and brass thimbles are difficult to date.

72 Victorian brass thimble inscribed 'Heroes of the Crimea'.
(Private collection)

Unlike silver thimbles they have no hallmarks and they are seldom engraved. There is no problem, however, over a Victorian commemorative brass thimble inscribed 'Heroes of the Crimea' which places it about 1855 or slightly later. The size of some Victorian brass thimbles suggests that they were intended for men's wear. Because silver was expensive, brass was widely used for the cheaper souvenir thimbles which carry the same sort of inscriptions such as 'Forget me not', 'Blessings attend you', 'Be merry and wise' and in German 'Lebe wohl'. Brass thimbles were also used for advertising before aluminium and plastics took over this field. The English soap manufacturers R. S. Hudson Ltd., who pioneered soap powders during the second half of the nineteenth century, made use of brass thimbles to promote their products in competition with other soap manufacturers such as Pears' Soap with whom they finally united in 1914 as part of the Lever Bros. concern. Thimbles similar to brass but of a redder hue are made of copper and are relatively scarce. Copper thimbles (or brass thimbles with a high proportion of copper) are in general well made and of more interest than the average brass thimble.

Possibly the most unusual use for thimbles arose in the United States during the early part of the nineteenth century when brass thimbles became an item of trade with the Indian tribes and many examples are reported to have been found on Indian sites which have small holes punched through the top so that the thimbles could be hung on thongs over a bead in the manner of a small bell. They were used to ornament clothing and a complete dress so ornamented may be seen in the Field Museum of Natural History at Chicago. The dress which originates from the Klamath Reservation is said to date back to about 1800 and it has 41 thimbles hanging from it as pendants, all unused, of different sizes and not identical. It can only be assumed that itinerant pedlars once visited that part of Oregon inhabited by the Klamath tribe and that the thimbles were traded and adapted for a purpose for which they were not intended. The use of thimble bells to adorn clothing is well attested and is a further instance if such were required of the vagaries of taste and fashion.

Brass thimbles continue to be manufactured in some quantities but chiefly for sale in the poorer and less developed countries where however they are meeting increased competition from thimbles made of plastics. In the United States and Western Europe, brass thimbles are very little used though they are still manufactured for special purposes, as in Spain where the so-called Toledo thimbles and thimbles of traditional Moorish pattern with imitation enamel are made for the tourist trade. Otherwise the brass thimble is fast disappearing and will soon become a rarity.

Other base metal thimbles

Whilst brass has long been the established favourite among base metals for the purposes of thimble manufacture, other metals have also been employed including iron which it is believed was used from earliest times. Unfortunately iron tends to rust and few examples have survived. Some very beautiful iron thimbles were made in Italy at the end of the seventeenth and the beginning of the eighteenth centuries which were decorated with flowers, leaves, birds and animals, all magnificently engraved and sometimes with gold inlay. A particularly fine collection may be found in the Musée Le Secq des Tournelles at Rouen (see illustration). These thimbles were very durable but they had the disadvantage of being heavy; those at the Musée Le Secq des Tournelles, for instance, weighing up to 17 grams as compared to 3 or 4 grams which is a fair average weight for a thimble. Neither is it surprising that 'Dame's thimmel' was so much dreaded since an iron thimble of this kind could evidently become a fearsome instrument of punishment.

In 1763 Parson Woodforde recorded in his Diary the gift to his sister of needles, pins and two steel thimbles which he had bought

73 Italian iron and steel thimbles from the seventeenth and eighteenth century.
(Musée Le Secq des Tournelles)

74 The use of steel to strengthen silver thimbles. Left to right: early nineteenth-century silver thimble with steel top (the use of steel-topped thimbles started during the eighteenth century); mid-nineteenth-century iron thimble with silver lining; mid-nineteenth-century silver thimble covered with steel cap; late nineteenth-century iron thimble with silver lining; late nineteenth-century silver thimble with steel core (see fig. 75). *(Private collection)*

75 Cross-section of Dorcas thimble. Note thin black line showing steel core between two layers of silver. *(Private collection)*

in Oxford. And in 1819 Messrs Rouy and Berthier exhibited at the Paris Exhibition of that date steel thimbles which the judges reported to be 'well made, well designed and free of the disadvantages attaching to thimbles of copper, gold, ivory, mother-of-pearl and wood'. Iron or steel thimbles are still available for heavy work such as upholstery but these are normally lined with a softer metal like silver, brass or a pewter-type alloy in order to make them more comfortable to wear on the finger. Iron or steel thimbles marked 'Iles' 'OA & S' or 'Abel Morrall' are of English manufacture.

Because iron is very resistant, a small iron or steel cap was often fitted to the tip of silver, brass and even sometimes gold thimbles to make them less susceptible to the wear of the needle. Such thimbles were made from the eighteenth century onwards until silver thimbles with a steel cap gave way to the silver thimble which is reinforced with a steel core. Collectors may come across thimbles of traditional English design which look like silver but which are abnormally heavy and which will be attracted by a magnet. They consist essentially of sterling silver sandwiched round an inner core of hardened steel and in consequence are extremely tough and durable; they are also better balanced than thimbles with steel tops as the weight is distributed evenly around the thimble. Since they include a steel core these thimbles cannot carry a hallmark but they may well carry the brand name 'Dura', 'Dreema', 'Dorcas' or 'Little Dorcas'. Others merely carry a size (or pattern) number. The 'Dreema' thimbles were manufactured by Henry Griffith of Leamington and the 'Dorcas' thimbles by Charles Horner of Halifax. Such thimbles are virtually indestructible, so much so that the Dorcas thimbles carried a guarantee, 'Exchanged free if rendered useless from any cause whatsoever'. The manufacture of silver thimbles with a steel core goes back to the late nineteenth century and possibly earlier. The price of Dorcas thimbles was quoted in an advertisement in a ladies' magazine in the 1880s at two shillings and six pence.

Going back to straightforward iron and steel thimbles, the more modern are made of plain sheeting or tinplate pressed or stamped into shape in much the same way as a modern brass thimble. Such thimbles are easily damaged, they are hard on the finger and despite various finishes designed to render them more attractive, they tend to deteriorate and become unsightly. One of the more common designs found is a somewhat elongated thimble with a plain rim and two or three tiers rising round the sides. Besides being used as thimbles, these were intended to act as the caps for small tubular containers enclosing needles and thread – or in other words small emergency sewing kits. These kits of varying designs and materials have long proved popular gifts and can also be very practical. They were standard issue in the British

76 Wooden sewing kit with metal cap designed to be used as a thimble.
(*Private collection*)

77 Iron with gold inlay – Spanish, probably early twentieth-century. Height 2·3 cm.
(*Private collection*)

78 Base metal thimbles. Left to right: design often found on thimbles of gold and silver, patented 28th May 1889, United States; another popular design, United States; flower and foliage border, continental; modified English motif; floral motif, unknown origin.
(*Private collection*)

Army during both world wars and were known to soldiers as 'house-wives'. It might surprise many ex-servicemen to know that this is not army slang but that the expression goes back to at least the eighteenth century. Readers of Jane Austen will recall that Mrs John Dashwood gave the Misses Steele 'huswifes' which are described elsewhere as 'nee-dle book(s) made by some emigrant'.[35] But going back to tubular con-tainers thimbles of this kind with two or three tiers designed to act as covers for a sewing kit are surprisingly common, more so in fact than the sewing kits themselves which are somewhat scarcer. Other types of iron thimbles will also be found but generally speaking they are of little interest. It need hardly be added that whilst it is often difficult to determine the metal of which a thimble is made, there is no difficulty here, since an iron or steel thimble will readily respond to a magnet.

More recently the white metal aluminium has been used extensively for making thimbles which have the dual advantage of being inexpensive and light on the finger. The difficulty is that aluminium tends to be so soft that the thimbles are easily damaged and wear out quickly. Thimble manufacturers have sought to remedy this by making thimbles of hardened aluminium and by introducing an iron tip. They have also sought to make their thimbles more colourful by giving them a tinted metallic finish. But aluminium thimbles have never proved very successful except for advertising for which purpose they have been pro-duced in enormous quantities. Otherwise with the exception of a few designs which aim to imitate the design of brass or silver thimbles, they tend to be rather dull and of only limited interest for the collector. In England the brand name 'Stratnoid' is associated with aluminium thimbles.

Nickel is another metal which has been used for thimble-making, especially in two main alloys.One is nickel silver, also known as German silver, which is an alloy of copper, nickel and zinc. Nickel silver is sometimes used as a base for silver plating; it looks like silver and its name is derived from the fact that it was developed in Germany. The other is cupro-nickel, a generic name used to describe a range of alloys composed, as the name implies, of copper and nickel in varying proportions. Cupro-nickel has a rather yellower, duller sheen than nickel silver. It is not known when cupro-nickel was first used for thimble-making but it was in use during the second half of the nineteenth century. The use of nickel silver appears to have come somewhat later though its properties were well known and electro-plating was actively pro-moted at the time of the Great Exhibition (1851). Nickel silver thimbles may be marked 'Solid nickel silver', 'nickel silver, sterling silver plated', 'nickel plated nickel silver' or other variations denoting the method

of manufacture. The leading brand names to be found on cupro-nickel and nickel silver thimbles in Great Britain are 'Iles', 'OA & S' (also 'OA & Co') and 'Abel Morrall'. There is also a maker's mark showing three thimbles in a shield. Thimbles made of nickel alloys were widely used for cheap souvenirs such as 'The Queen's Record Thimble, the best of all', 'Victoria Jubilee' with a crown, and more recently thimbles issued to commemorate the coronation of King George VI and that of Queen Elizabeth II. Nickel alloys were also used for advertising, notably by the Prudential Life Insurance and also by Abel Morrall themselves who provided a thimble urging housewives to 'use Morrall's needles'. Thimbles marked 'Corozo silver' are late Victorian and are made of cupro-nickel. Several patented thimbles were produced in nickel alloys including Iles' patent ventilated thimble and also an Iles model with a celluloid skirting. A thumb-shaped thimble (British Patent No. 19157) was produced in nickel silver and another, the 'threader thimble' made of nickel plated nickel silver had a threader attachment and retailed together with thimble case and instructions at two shillings and threepence. The design of thimbles made of nickel alloys is often plain and uninspired but among the more interesting designs should be mentioned a cupro-nickel thimble with a regular dodecagonal skirting (Rd. No. 108544) and another with an early railway scene milled round the base. The latter is a duplicate of an identical silver thimble dating back to early Victorian times and it suggests that the use of cupro-nickel for thimble-making may be older than might otherwise appear.

Silver being relatively inexpensive, there is little incentive for base metal thimbles to be silver plated and passed off as silver. Nevertheless care should be taken when purchasing so-called engraved or chased silver thimbles of artisan manufacture in Iran or other Middle Eastern countries as these may be found to be made of base metal with a silver coating. More interestingly there is at least one English model which from its appearance and weight may be thought to be a typical steel-cored silver thimble but which is in fact made of silver plated copper. Steel-cored thimbles do not carry a sterling mark and outwardly there is no difference. Yellow metal thimbles are sometimes given a light silver-plating but this is more in the nature of a finish and is readily recognisable. The following extract from the Harrod's Catalogue for 1895 may be of interest as illustrating the items carried by a London store and the relative prices:

Harrod's Stores Limited, Brompton
Haberdashery
No. 17 Department – Ground Floor

Thimbles
Steel per dozen $0/10\frac{3}{4}$
Plated per dozen $0/10\frac{3}{4}$
Silver plated each $0/4\frac{3}{4}$
Silver lined each $0/6\frac{3}{4}$
Sterling silver each $1/3\frac{1}{2}$
Plated, enamel lined each $0/10\frac{3}{4}$

More expensive thimbles including gold thimbles would no doubt have been available from the jewellery department. At about the same time in 1897, the Sears Roebuck catalogue in the United States featured thimbles as follows:

Aluminium thimbles 1 cent each, German silver thimbles 3 cents, solid silver 20 cents, with border 30 cents, engraved 45 cents, hand engraved 55 cents; gold filled 75 cents, engraved warranted $1.15; solid gold 10 carat $1.90.

Various other metals and alloys have been used for the purpose of thimble manufacturing, some of which such as pinchbeck and Prince's metal have already been considered. It is possible that thimbles have been made of pewter which is an alloy of four parts of tin and one part of lead but their existence needs to be verified.

Base metals do not have the same appeal as gold and silver so that thimbles made of base metals have tended to be neglected. They are also difficult to date and to classify. Nevertheless base metal thimbles have always played an important role and it should be remembered that with the advent of the sewing-machine and the development of plastics, metal thimbles as we know them are rapidly becoming obsolete. In the same way as the many millions of brass thimbles which were made over the centuries have mostly disappeared, so will their modern counterparts unless they are put aside and cared for – and what better way than by collecting now what is likely to be the rarity of the future.

80 Plastic thimbles. Left to right: Early plastic, about 1900; the Cupid, decorated with transfer design, about 1920; pink coloured finger and nail, modern; decorated with hand-painted flowers, about 1930; flame-proof, modern.
(*Private collection*)

81 Japanese plastic sewing rings.
(*Private collection*)

Plastic thimbles

The use of plastics for making thimbles is older than is sometimes recognised. The invention of celluloid during the nineteenth century was followed by the development of products such as casein and others which were soon used by the thimble industry. In 1905 H. M. Arpiarian patented (British patent No. 21630) the manufacture of thimbles made of vulcanite which were to remain so malleable that after a short time they would become bedded to the fingers of the users. More practical, in 1908 C. E. Iles patented (British patent No. 1149) the lining of thimbles with sheet celluloid or like material. But it was not until the First World War that plastic thimbles really came into their own. Early plastic thimbles are sometimes mistaken for ivory or bone but although the colour may be similar, the finish is different and moreover plastic thimbles often carry a size number either on the outside round the rim or else inside at the apex.

During the inter-war years, plastic thimbles were sometimes hand-painted round the rim with posies or other flower decorations. 'Halex' is a brand name occasionally encountered on thimbles decorated in this way. Others were decorated with a transfer design 'Forget-me-not' with a garland of the flowers of that name or 'The Cupid' with cherubs and garlands of roses.

The development of the plastics industry after the Second World War gave further impetus to the use of plastic thimbles. Sewing having lost much of the importance it once had, few women bother to buy a silver let alone a gold thimble and many make do with a plastic thimble which is both cheap and expendable. Plastic thimbles are now available in many different colours and varieties. They may embody various features such as stepped rings or helical spirals inside the thimble to give a better grip or they may be made of flame proof plastics as a safety factor. The design of plastic thimbles, however, tends to be conservative and they invariably have a squarish cross-section and flattened top. In the United States plastic thimbles are used extensively for advertising (see Advertising thimbles, p. 115 below).

In Japan where it is customary to sew with the side of the finger, there are plastic ring-type thimbles. These are made in two parts consisting of an adjustable band of leather or plastic which fits round the finger and holds in place a small shield of hardened plastic which is the part which actually protects the finger from the head of the needle. Alternatively they consist more simply of an expandable plastic ring with overlapping ends and an indented front section.

Very rough and ill-finished plastic thimbles are sometimes made as tokens or cheap gifts for Christmas crackers and the like.

Tailors' thimbles

Historical evidence suggests that the ring-type thimble with an open top such as is used by tailors may have pre-dated the domed type of thimble. Not only were many Roman thimbles designed to be used sideways but Roman ring-type thimbles have often been found, e.g. in the ruins of Herculaneum. What is more, there is good reason to believe that the early leather thimbles or fingerlings consisted essentially of a strip of leather sewn into the form of a ring and worn round the finger or thumb.

With the increasing use of metal thimbles and the development of sharper and finer needles, ring-type thimbles have tended to disappear. In Europe nowadays their use is confined to tailors or to upholsterers who still find a ring-type thimble more convenient for their type of work which necessitates a good deal of hard sewing. For normal sewing, however, the pressure exerted with the tip of the finger is sufficient and the use of the domed type thimble is now universal. Nevertheless there are individuals who still prefer to sew sideways and it is by no means uncommon to find a domed type thimble which is heavily worn round the sides, showing that it has been used consistently in this way. In the Far East the ring-type thimble is still widely used, plastic or metal ring-type thimbles are readily available in the shops and purchased in preference to the domed type. Ring-type thimbles are also used in China.

It is noteworthy that in some countries the word for a tailor's thimble is distinct from that for an ordinary thimble, which emphasises the essential difference in their development. The German language,

82 Heavy duty tailors' thimbles. Left to right: iron with lead lining, nineteenth-century; brass, nineteenth-century; iron with white metal lining by Abel Morrall; iron with brass lining; brass. Tailors' thimbles are difficult to date as the design has remained largely unchanged for the last hundred years or more.
(Private collection)

for instance, distinguishes between the 'Fingerhut' which is the normal type of thimble and the 'Nähring' or sewing-ring. In Italy, whereas the word 'ditale' is used currently throughout the country, in Tuscany a thimble is known as an 'anello' (de cucire) or in other words a ring. This distinction extends even to the Eskimos who differentiate between 'tikerk', a normal domed type thimble and 'pudjortok', a tailor's thimble.

   Another feature is that whereas domed type thimbles are often decorated and otherwise embellished and made of precious metals, this does not apply to the ring-type thimble which has always maintained its characteristics as a workaday sewing-tool. Ring-type thimbles are normally made of iron or brass and more recently plastics, but it is unusual to find ring-type thimbles made of plain silver let alone anything more expensive. This would seem to confirm that the ring-type thimble was essentially suited and designed for rough work and that the change-over to the domed type thimble has been associated with the development of finer and more delicate needlework.

   At the other extreme, for really heavy sewing such as sailmaking or leather work, a palm protector is used in preference to a thimble. It will be recalled that in Rudyard Kipling's *Captains Courageous,* 'Harvey spent his leisure hours ... learning to use a needle and palm'. The sailor's palm was already well known in the seventeenth century when it even featured in a naval dictionary: 'The palm is formed of a piece of leather or canvas, on the middle of which is fixed a round plate of iron of an inch in diameter, whose surface is pierced with a number of small holes to catch the head of the sail needle. The leather is formed so as to encircle the hand and button on the back thereof, while the iron remains in the palm.'[36] The buttons have been discarded in favour of laces but otherwise the modern palm protector remains substantially unchanged.

83 Ring-type thimbles. Left to right: Brass, China, nineteenth-century; brass, unknown origin; silver, United States; plastic, Japan, modern; chromium plate, Japan, modern. *(Private collection)*

Children's thimbles

It is not so long ago that sewing ranked with the three R's and that little girls vied with each other in the fineness of their samplers. Sewing lessons began as soon as the child could hold a needle and specially small thimbles were needed to fit on small fingers. These were sometimes made in 'sets' consisting of three thimbles of increasing sizes allowing for the growth of the small needlewoman. A pretty thimble might be the reward for good work at school or might be a birthday or confirmation gift. These would usually be of silver or brass but more rarely there might also be the promise of a real gold thimble. Children's thimbles in gold are difficult to find but a delightful example decorated with alternate pearls and beads of pink coral is illustrated. It is hard to imagine a more charming and tasteful gift for a young lady.

All small thimbles are not necessarily children's thimbles. Very small thimbles – far too small to fit even a child's finger – were made as charms to hang on bracelets; others were made for use in the doll's house and a third category served as tokens for children's games, the latter usually made of base metal and inscribed 'For a good girl'. These should not be confused with genuine children's thimbles which normally closely resemble the thimbles worn by grown-ups and like them are often engraved or otherwise decorated round the base. Small silver thimbles of a size suitable for children were also designed for use as pudding charms.

84 Gold – alternate coral and pearl setting, a young girl's thimble. English, late nineteenth-century. Height 2·0 cm.
(Private collection)

85 Children's thimbles. Left to right: steel-topped English, early nineteenth-century; adult's silver thimble for comparison, height 2·4 cm.; gold, French, nineteenth-century; silver, French, nineteenth-century; silver, Portugal (Oporto), early twentieth-century; silver, English, about 1850; doll's silver thimble, height 0·8 cm.; ivory, early nineteenth-century.
(Private collection)

Souvenir thimbles

Ever since the seventeenth century and almost certainly before, royal events have inspired the production of souvenir or commemorative thimbles, the earliest recorded examples being two silver thimbles with medallion portraits of Charles II and Queen Catherine of Braganza which are in the safe-keeping of the British Museum and the London Museum respectively. However it was not until the end of the eighteenth century and the beginning of the nineteenth that improved methods of manufacture made it possible to produce large numbers of specially designed thimbles at a relatively low price and that the souvenir thimble as such really came into its own. In Britain during the reign of Queen Victoria, royal weddings, royal births and other royal occasions inspired countless designs and among the chief events commemorated in this way during the nineteenth century are the following:

Coronation of Queen Victoria	1837
Wedding of Queen Victoria and Prince Albert	1840
Birth of Prince of Wales	1841
Queen Victoria's visit to Ireland	1849
Death of Wellington	1852
Queen Victoria Golden Jubilee	1887
Queen Victoria Diamond Jubilee	1897

86 English commemorative silver thimbles – Left to right: Wedding of Queen Victoria, 1840; Birth of Prince of Wales, 1841; Diamond Jubilee, 1897 (Reg. design No. 295282); Coronation of George V, 1937; Coronation of George VI, 1937; Coronation of Queen Elizabeth II, 1953 (hallmark includes Queen's profile struck on all silver made in England and Scotland in 1952 and 1953). *(Private collection)*

So popular did souvenir thimbles become during the reign of Queen Victoria that they were produced on the occasion of many minor functions to record visits by royalty or the opening of new enterprises.

The practice of designing souvenir thimbles for royal occasions is still followed in England and such thimbles were produced on the occasion of the Silver Jubilee of King George V in 1935, the Coronation of King George VI in 1937 and the Coronation of Queen Elizabeth II in 1953. Souvenir thimbles were also produced to commemorate the investiture of the Prince of Wales in 1969 and the wedding of H.R.H. Princess Anne in 1973. Most souvenir thimbles are made of silver but they have also been produced in cupro-nickel and other base metal. Gold souvenir thimbles may occasionally be found.

The great revolution in modes of travel at the beginning of the nineteenth century sparked off a fashion for tourism and sightseeing. Until then the only form of transport was on horseback or by coach so that the mass of the people rarely travelled away from home. The railways changed all this by allowing more and more people to travel to more and more places. The souvenir trade boomed and at a time when holiday snaps or even more elaborate photographic records of interesting places visited by tourists, still lay in the future, there was an immediate and heavy demand for small inexpensive objects as mementoes of holidays and sightseeing trips. In an age when household sewing was still an important activity, thimbles and thimble cases were an obvious choice and some very fine silver thimbles were produced decorated round the base below the indentations with views of famous landmarks or places of historical interest. Unfortunately silver wears easily and the design may lose definition but in good condition thimbles of this kind can be very attractive. The following are among those which occur most frequently: Balmoral (from 1848), Great Exhibition (1851), Dover Castle, Windsor Castle, London Bridge, St. Paul's Cathedral, Royal Pavilion Brighton, Buckingham Palace, Tower of London, Tay Bridge (1877-1879).

In the United States souvenir thimbles did not catch on to the same extent. Simons Brothers produced some commemorative thimbles including one depicting the driving of the 'Golden Spike' and there is a thimble commemorating the Chicago 'World Colombian Exposition 1492-1892' which was held on the occasion of the 400th anniversary of the discovery of America. But otherwise American souvenir or commemorative thimbles were comparatively rare until recently when the fashion for thimble collecting and the forthcomming celebration of the bicentenary of American Independence has led to a crop of new designs for sale to collectors. Already the following are reported: Liberty Bell Bicentennial Thimble – Made in USA; George and Martha Washington

Thimble – Made in Great Britain; Betsy Ross Bicentennial Thimble – Made in Holland; Bicentennial Statue of Liberty Thimble – Made in France.

The situation in continental Europe evolved somewhat differently and during the second half of the nineteenth century, thimbles were sold in many of the leading spas and holiday resorts which were essentially of traditional design but which bore the name of the locality. In Germany for instance, thimbles of traditional design with stone tops were produced both for the home market, e.g. Heidelberg, Wiesbaden, etc., and for the export trade including Russia where in Czarist days souvenir thimbles were not uncommon. In Britain however, with the notable exception of the Isle of Man where about 1895 souvenir thimbles of this type appear to have been popular, they only had a limited success.. This may have been due to the fact that souvenir thimble cases made of wood and decorated with transfer scenes of holiday resorts were widely available between 1860 and 1900, and that a souvenir thimble as such was possibly superfluous. Be that as it may, few English thimbles bear the name or designation of a locality until 1930 when the well-known English jewellers and goldsmiths Henry Griffith and Sons of Leamington Spa manufactured a series of plain thimbles of

87 Souvenir thimbles. Left to right: Isle of Man, 1909; German-made thimble inscribed in cyrillic characters and exported for sale to foreign tourists in Russia, late nineteenth-century; Near East, inscribed in Arabic characters; Russian niello silver inscribed 'Caucasus', late nineteenth-century; unusually designed English silver thimble inscribed 'Wiesbaden', 1909. *(Private collection)*

traditional English pattern with the names of various towns and seaside-resorts in a milled band situated below the indentations. Sold at one shilling each, all the following places were represented by such named thimbles:

Aberdovey	Eastbourne	Peebles
Aberystwith	Edinburgh	Penzance
Aylesbury	Felixstowe	Portsmouth
Babbacombe	Glastonbury	Sandown
Birmingham	Gravesend	St. Leonards
Blackpool	Guernsey	Scarborough
Bridlington	Halifax	Shrewsbury
Brighton	Inverness	Skegness
Bristol	Jersey	Southend-on-Sea
Bude	Killarney	Southsea
Chatham	Leamington Spa	Stratford-on-Avon
Chester	Llandudno	Teignmouth
Colchester	London	Tenby
Colwyn Bay	Minehead	Wallesey
Combe Martin	Newquay	Westcliffe-on-Sea
Croydon	Omagh	Whitley Bay
Dewsbury	Oxford	York

Henry Griffith and Sons manufactured these thimbles in considerable quantities under the brand name 'The Spa' before discontinuing their production two or three years later. At least one other firm sought to follow their example but presumably with little success since specimens are scarce. Henry Griffith also manufactured souvenir thimbles for sale on the P & O liners sailing between Great Britain and Australia. Some of these bore the following names: S.S. *Orion*, S.S. *Orontes*, S.S. *Oronsay*, S.S. *Orsova*. A ship's souvenir thimble was also made carrying the name of R.M.S. *Britannic*.

Whilst the manufacture of souvenir thimbles has largely been discontinued in Great Britain, on the Continent they continue to be sold in many countries. Possibly the most widespread are enamelled silver thimbles with simulated stone tops which can be purchased in many tourist centres. They are manufactured in Germany and carry a printed or transfer view of some well-known monument with the name of the town concerned on the back, among them the following: Parthenon – Athens; Columbus Monument – Barcelona; Puerta del Sol – Madrid; Duomo – Milan; St. Peters – Rome.

Another series made of electro-plated nickel silver or other base metal carries an enamelled shield displaying the arms of the locality

88 Silver thimble inscribed Leamington Spa, 1930. (*Private collection*)

or else a pictorial view of it. Among the places represented in this series are Copacabana, Rio de Janeiro, Puerto Rico, Titisee and Vereeniging.

Several countries produce thimbles of a distinctive pattern which although they do not carry any definite written or pictorial reference are nevertheless destined essentially for the tourist trade. Greece is a case in point and the small, rounded, dome-shaped thimbles with traditional Greek ornamentation are made mainly as souvenirs. So are the Mexican silver thimbles which are sold in many different patterns to American tourists. And so are many of the Spanish thimbles including the so-called Toledo thimbles made of yellow metal with a dark brown band round the rim. Another well-known item is the 'Monumento de la Linea Equinoccial' silver thimble from Ecuador.

If the above are mostly commonplace, there are older and more interesting continental souvenir thimbles to be found, such as for instance the Russian niello-decorated thimbles which in Czarist times were

89 Religious thimbles. Left to right: white metal, Sacred Heart; plated brass, Sainte Thérèse, France; silver, unknown Madonna, South America; silver, Virgin del Pilar, Spain; white metal, Basilica de Fatima, Portugal; white metal, unknown Madonna, France. (*Private collection*)

sold to tourists in the Caucasus. Not so rare but also very attractive are niello thimbles from the Middle East with riverside scenes and others featuring pyramids, mosques and feluccas.

Another interesting type of souvenir thimble is associated with pilgrimages. In many Catholic countries it was customary for suitably designed thimbles to commemorate shrines and holy places. Among these may be noted Notre Dame de Lourdes, Sainte Thérèse de l'Enfant Jésus at Lisieux, the Basilica of Fatima and La Virgen del Pilar Zaragossa. Thimbles with a religious motif but of more general appeal were also available. This custom has declined, but in a country such as Portugal thimbles with a religious motif are still very much in evidence.

It will be appreciated that thimbles were frequently sold in specially designed souvenir thimble cases and as such were sold as souvenirs even though the thimble itself was a normal straightforward thimble without special markings. This happened a great deal in Britain, for instance, where Scottish woodware thimble cases would be sold with a plain silver thimble, and also in central Europe where hand-carved wooden thimble cases were sold in large quantities to tourists.

In conclusion it is necessary to recall that thimbles were traditionally offered as personal mementoes and keepsakes and in this sense were often regarded as souvenirs. Collectors will know that thimbles are often engraved with names, dates and other fragments which no doubt meant a great deal to both the donor and the recipient but whose meaning was essentially personal and has necessarily been lost. More interesting from the collector's point of view are those thimbles which were specially designed as keepsakes such as, for instance, Victorian thimbles engraved 'Forget me not', or the more modern thimbles engraved 'For Auld Lang Syne' or 'Good Luck to You'. These somewhat banal phrases find their echo on the Continent, be it 'Recordaçao' in Portugal, 'Souvenir' in France or 'Bin ich deine' in Germany. There are many such thimbles from many different countries, but customs have changed and the gift of a thimble as a memento or keepsake is now largely a thing of the past.

Advertising thimbles

Thimbles bearing the name or designation of the donor have been used extensively for advertising particularly in the United States. Such thimbles are normally made of some cheap material such as aluminium or plastic, though advertising thimbles of brass and also silver are by no means uncommon.

The evidence available suggests that the use of thimbles as a means of advertising started during the nineteenth century and that the earliest thimbles of this kind were made of silver. Such thimbles were relatively valuable and might be produced for the purposes of a sales campaign such as that of the silver Lipton Tea thimbles which were available in exchange for a given number of Lipton Tea packet labels. Other well-known products which have silver·thimbles bearing their name include Andrews Liver Salt, Hovis Bread, Lifebuoy Soap, Quaker Oats and Heinz 57 Varieties. Several English jewellers, notably James Walker, stocked silver thimbles bearing their name which they used to offer as a gift to accompany the purchase of a wedding ring.

The use of brass thimbles for advertising dates from about the turn of the century. Various products have been advertised by means of brass thimbles and more particularly sewing requisites such as 'Alderman Sewing Silk', 'Barbour's Linen Thread', 'Câblé Louis d'Or' and 'Gütermann's Sewing Silk'. Other miscellaneous products such as 'Lutona Cocoa', 'Chaussures Bailly' and 'C.W.S. Tea' were also advertised. The manufacturers of Hudson's Soap were more ambitious. They brought out a brass sewing-kit consisting of a small needle case acting

90 Metal sewing kit inscribed 'Hudson's Soap'. *(Private collection)*

91 Advertising thimbles.
Left to right: aluminium,
'Lyons Cakes', on blue
ground; aluminium, 'Nestlé's
Milk is richest in cream', on
black ground; aluminium,
'Use Dr Lovelace's Soap', on
red ground; aluminium, Use
C.W.S. Congress Soap on
blackground with needle-
threading device; aluminium,
Byrd for Governor', printed
design, United States; yellow
plastic, 'The United Savings
Association', United States.
(*Private collection*)

as the spindle for two reels of cotton, contained in a small cylindrical tube closed at one end and the other end capped by a thimble with the words 'Hudson's Soap' round the rim.

Aluminium, being a soft metal, is not really suitable for making thimbles because it does not stand up to wear and tear. Nevertheless the very softness of aluminium means that it can be used to stamp out thimbles cheaply and in quantities at very low cost. The advertisement normally appears in raised letters on the side and there is a coloured band – red, green, blue or black being the favourite colours – which serves to offset the lettering though this is still legible after the paint has worn off. More rarely the lettering has no coloured background or else the advertisement is printed with a special type of ink direct on the alumium. Aluminium thimbles may have a simulated stone top for added strength, the more common colours being blue, green, red and amber. They may also have a needle threading attachment. Many household products have been advertised in this way and the following is a list of some British firms and/or products which may be found advertised on aluminium thimbles:

Absolom's Tea
Albion Calf Meal
Andrews Liver Salt
Bermaline Bread
Bisto Meat Dishes
Blue Star Margarine
Centurion Enamel Paint
Clean Hands
Colman's Custard and Mustard
Crawford's Cream Crackers
Crawford's Biscuits
Crumpsall Cream Crackers
C.W.S. Congress Soap
Dr. Lovelace's Soap
Dysons Self-Raising Flour
Edwards' Desiccated Soup
Epp's Cocoa
Equitable Life Ins. Co.
Featherstones
Gas for Economy
Golden Stream Tea
Goodwin's Sheffield Tools
Home and Colonial
Home Notes
Horrockses Fashions
H.P. Sauce

Hudson's Soap
Jacksons' Footwear
Jacksons' Hats and Boots
John West Salmon
King Human Hair
Lyons' Cakes
Lyons' Green Label Tea
Macleod's Household Soap
Macleod's Tea
Mother Seigel's Syrup
Natural Health Salts
Nestlé's Milk
News of the World
Nugget Boot Polishes
Reid's Stout
Sainsbury's of Lewisham
Scowborough's Nourishing Ale
Sparva
Spencer's Jewellery
Swift's Plate Beef
Symington's Coffee
Vilene Interlining
Weldons Fashions
Yorkshire Evening News
Zebra Grate Polish
Zwicky Silk

No doubt there are many others. Aluminium advertising thimbles have also been used extensively in the United States, so much so that it would be impractical to attempt to list known varieties. The use of aluminium thimbles for advertising does not appear to have been so widespread on the Continent though they are by no means unusual, e.g. the German 'Waschpulver Blanca' and 'Gritzner' sewing machines.

Advertising thimbles made of aluminium are suitable for collection but only if in mint condition. Damaged aluminium thimbles are unsightly and best avoided.

In the United States plastic thimbles have also proved very popular for advertising purposes and to some extent have displaced aluminium thimbles. They are made in a wide variety of colours and used to advertise many different products and services. They have even been used for the purpose of promoting political candidates during election campaigns, including the former President Nixon himself when he was seeking election as Senator. The use of plastic thimbles for advertising is largely confined to North America.

Finger guards

Thimble collectors will occasionally find a small silver appliance resembling a ring, one side being perhaps an inch wide and curled at the top and the other not much wider than an ordinary finger ring. This is a finger guard (also known as a finger shield or finger protector), and was worn in the days before sewing-machines when much plain sewing and hemming had to be done by hand. It fitted on the first finger of the left hand. The material would be held between the thumb and the tip of the finger in such a way that the part of the material to be sewn rested on the metal and the finger was thus protected from the needle point. Finger guards are no longer used and there are not many people today who would even recognise one, but in Victorian times they were commonplace. Any well-fitted needlework box included both a thimble to protect the middle finger on the right hand from the blunt end of the needle and a finger guard to protect the first finger of the left hand from its point. They were usually made of silver and sometimes of silver-gilt, gold or ivory.

Silver finger guards seldom carry a hallmark though they sometimes carry a maker's mark, notably that of Joseph Taylor of Birmingham (IT) who was active in the late eighteenth and early nineteenth century. An amusing novelty dating from about that period consists of a needle cushion mounted on a silver base on which screws a finger

92 Unusually finely decorated silver finger guard. Probably early Victorian. Height 2·4 cm. (*Private collection*)

guard and then a thimble. The underside served as a letter seal after the fashion of the time. Some finger guards covered the finger more extensively than others and in extreme cases the finger would be almost completely enclosed. Finger guards were not as ornate as thimbles, probably because ornamentation was likely to catch the point of the needle, but they are not all necessarily plain and some finely engraved specimens may occasionally be found. The more ornate finger guards tend to be somewhat later and as a general guide the plainer the finger guard, the earlier it is likely to be.

More recently the finger guard has given way to the imitation tortoise-shell or celluloid finger protector but these are also becoming obsolete in an age when almost all plain sewing is done by machine.

93 Silver finger guards of varying design. Mostly mid-nineteenth-century. *(Private collection)*

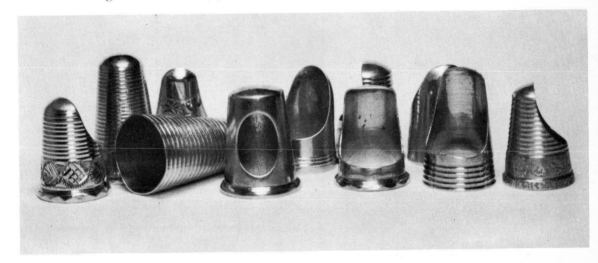

94 Imitation tortoise-shell finger protector. *(Private collection)*

Just a thimbleful

It has long been the practice to make small cups and measures in the form of a thimble and Sylvia Groves illustrates a commemorative cup of this kind (see Bibliography, p. 146). It is about five inches high and was probably one of a set made on behalf of the Tailor's Guild of Nuremberg in 1586. It is of silver plated brass and is a close replica of the silver thimbles which were used on the Continent at the time. There is a similar cup in the Berlin Kunstgewerbemuseum which is of gold plated copper and is inscribed 'Vivat Die Ehrsame Schneiderzunft' or 'Long live the worshipful guild of tailors' and is dated 1601.

It is probable that some early pewter measures were made in the form of a thimble. Certainly the thimble was already accepted as an indication of measure – witness the directions in a military manual dated 1617: 'Take half a thimbleful of Gunpowder' (Markham – Cavalry II). And Dryden somewhat less prosaically wrote: 'Yes, and measure for measure, too, Sosia; that is a thimbleful of gold, a thimbleful of love.' (Amphitryon).

During Victorian times such thimbles made of pewter or slag glass were popular novelties bearing the inscription 'Just a thimbleful' meaning a very little drop – usually of spirits. 'Only a thimble' is sometimes used in common parlance in place of a thimbleful. Thomas Hood wrote in 'A Tale of a Trumpet':

> Tis true to her cottage still they came …
> And never swallow'd a thimble the less
> Of something the Reader is left to guess.

In more recent times outsize porcelain thimbles have been made as decorations or sold as souvenirs. There are many examples among the Goss or Arcadia ware decorated with miscellaneous coats-of-arms including the arms of seaside resorts where they were sold before the first World War. Unlike the older pewter measures which are comparatively rare, Goss and Arcadia heraldic ware thimbles are inexpensive and quite collectable. There are also some smaller Goss thimbles, handpainted and only slightly larger than life size which were not intended for practical use but merely for decoration.

Electroplated spirit measures in the form of a thimble also occur. These mostly belong to the twentieth century and are sold as bar accessories.

95 Thimble shapes and spirit measures. Left to right: Scottish spirit measure in the form of a thistle; Arcadia porcelain inscribed Windsor; Victorian slag glass; Carlton porcelain with arms of King Edward VII; nickel-plated spirit measure; pewter spirit measure.
(*Private collection*)

96 Steel thimble holder from a chatelaine, late nineteenth-century.
(*Private collection*)

Thimble cases

It is by no means certain when special cases were first made to hold thimbles. There are references to caskets of wood, leather and crystal containing thimbles in the inventories of the fifteenth and sixteenth century but such caskets were not necessarily thimble cases in the sense employed here, namely that of a small decorated container specially designed to hold a thimble and nothing more. It can however be inferred that the jewellers and goldsmiths who lavished their art on decorating and embellishing thimbles from the fourteenth century onwards must almost certainly have designed suitable cases to match.

By the eighteenth century the more expensive thimbles were normally presented in a thimble case. Such cases might be egg-shaped made of multicoloured gold or of enamel to house an enamel thimble. Alternatively they might be made of gold-mounted ivory. More commonly the thimble might be presented in a small leather casket or a casket made of shagreen (galuchat) a material which was very much in vogue during the second half of the eighteenth century. There followed a range of thimble cases in ivory, tortoise-shell and mother-of-pearl, the latter being particularly popular in France about 1810 (Palais Royal). Thereafter the production of thimble cases increased enormously due to the demand for souvenirs and novelties; they were manufactured in a profusion of shapes, designs and materials which, if nothing else, is a tribute to Victorian versatility and imagination.

A different form of thimble case arose as a fitment (thimble-holder) for the chatelaines (or ménagères) which ladies carried hooked at their waist. In earlier times, pockets were non-existent and it was customary for the lady of the house to carry various items, notably her keys, hanging by a cord attached to the waistband. Subsequently the chatelaine was developed as an article of fashion, sometimes to carry a watch, watchkey and seal and sometimes to carry sewing implements including a thimble in a separate thimble holder. Changes in the style of clothing towards the end of the eighteenth century led to the wearing of the chatelaines being abandoned and it was not revived until the end of the nineteenth century when for a brief period there was a fashion for housewives to carry their keys attached to the waistband together with a chatelaine for holding sewing instruments. Thimble holders from this period, mostly silver, steel or other base metal, are not uncommon. In their simplest form they consist of a small bucket with a fabric lining, usually dark blue or purple, which served to hold the thimble. Others have a lid fitted with a hinge. Many were attached to the chatelaine by a small chain. Silver thimble holders can be elaborate with fine design and workmanship (Plate 2, p. 40). English thimble holders of this period

were mostly made in and around Birmingham and among the makers'
marks that of George Unite figures prominently.

Deserving of special notice and somewhat pre-dating the Victorian period, are the early English Tunbridge ware thimble cases in the
form of an egg made of natural wood, polished or varnished and more
often than not decorated with oil-paint – red, yellow and green usually
being the predominant colours. These were sold between 1790 and 1820
and it is possible to find wooden thimbles of about the same period
and manufacture. Somewhat later there followed thimble cases also
made at Tunbridge Wells of the type known as stickware. In this process
sticks of varying natural woods but of contrasting colours are glued
together into a block and turned on a lathe, the pattern depending
on the depth of cutting and the wood involved. These are also in the
shape of an egg or they may sometimes be acorn-shaped with the body

97 Early Tunbridge thimble
case. About 1820.
(Private collection)

98 Tunbridge stickware
thimble cases. About 1840.
(Private collection)

of plain wood and the screw-on top made of stickware. Thimbles were also made of stickware but they are somewhat rarer and difficult to find.

Following on Tunbridge ware came the development of Scottish woodware, also known as Mauchline ware because for a long time production was concentrated on Mauchline, a small town in Ayrshire. There are two kinds: the older is clan tartan ware which was first produced in the 1820s and consists of paper decorated with clan tartans and glued to wood – usually sycamore. So perfectly was the gluing done that it is almost impossible to tell the joints. Thimble cases were produced in many different shapes and many different clan tartans and in common with most clan tartan ware, were sold chiefly in Scotland. The more recent kind is transfer ware which was again usually sycamore and was decorated with transferred engravings. It was first introduced in the 1830s and remained popular until towards the turn of the century, though one factory remained in production until as late as 1933. Transfer ware was basically intended to simulate pen and ink drawings to meet the demand for cheap souvenirs. Some of the designs are very delicate and faithfully record the scenery and fashions at the time. Transfer ware thimble cases were normally decorated with engravings of places of historical interest or of the emerging holiday resorts such as the following: Alexandra Palace, Bournemouth from Terrace Mount, Trinity Gateway – Cambridge, Cowes – Isle of Wight, Douglas Iron Pier – Isle of Man, Edinburgh Castle, Marine Parade – Folkestone, Eversfield Place – Hastings, Llangollen and Castle Dinas Hill, The Mansion House, Peel Castle – Isle of Man, The Citadel – Plymouth, Saltburn-on-Sea, Sir Walter Scott Memorial, Swansea Pier, The Tower of

99 Tartan ware thimble cases.
(Private collection)

London, The Pier – Weston Super Mare, St. George's Park – Yarmouth.

There are of course countless others but the above will serve to give some idea of their variety. Transfer ware thimble cases were sold for export to France (e.g. La Colonne de la Grande Armée Boulogne-sur-Mer, Plage de St. Malo Marée Basse, etc.), to the United States (e.g. The Washington Monument – Washington D.C.) and to Australia. Thimble cases in both tartan ware and transfer ware are relatively common and occur in many different shapes and sizes.

100 Transfer ware thimble cases.
(Private collection)

101 Carved wood thimble holder in the shape of an edelweiss. Northern Alps, late nineteenth-century.
(Private collection)

102 Carved wood thimble holder in the shape of a bear. Northern Alps, late nineteenth-century.
(Private collection)

Wooden thimble cases were also made on the Continent, chiefly in Switzerland, Southern Germany and the Tyrol where wood carving was always an important cottage industry practised during the winter months when outdoor occupations were at a standstill. Thimble cases in the shape of a walnut, pine cone or mushroom are typical of this work. So too are thimble stands, popular until very recently, where the thimble rests on the carving of an edelweiss, eagle, bear or other object with a local association. A tourist item made in Hitler's Germany was a miniature walking boot and in it a silver thimble worked with swastikas.

Going back to the early nineteenth century, some reference has already been made to thimble cases of tortoise-shell and mother-of-pearl. These are normally of two kinds. One consists of a small rectangular casket $1\frac{1}{2}$ inches long by about 1 inch wide which is made of wood with a hinged lid. The casket is overlaid with mother-of-pearl and abalone in varying patterns and the inside is trimmed with velvet with the edgings finished in bone. The other kind consists of a small octagonal box about an inch across of similar construction and overlaid with

103 Gold thimble with original tortoise-shell casket. English, nineteenth-century. *(Private collection)*

104 Mother-of-pearl casket. English, nineteenth-century. *(Private collection)*

105 Victorian beadwork
thimble cases. At centre,
thimble and needle case combined.
(Private collection)

106 Vegetable ivory thimble
cases with matching thimbles.
English, mid-nineteenth-century.
(Private collection)

mother-of-pearl or abalone. This kind of casket was also veneered with tortoise-shell. Both are attractive but as in all delicate objects of this nature, condition is important and really ·fine specimens are comparatively rare.

Thimble cases made of Victorian bead-work were also popular and can be very attractive. These are normally made in two halves which screw together in the shape of an egg and the case itself is made of ivory. Occasionally the case is fitted with a small cylindrical container which projects at one end to hold needles, and is also covered in bead-work. Unfortunately bead-work is easily damaged and here again specimens in really fine condition are rare.

Many thimble cases during the Victorian era were made of vegetable ivory. This substance, which is often confused with bone, horn or real ivory but which can be distinguished by its somewhat oily feel and also by its obvious vegetable appearance where it is unpolished, comes from a South American tree *(Phytelephas macrocarpa)* which is allied to the palm. The hardened albumen of its seed called Corozo nut or ivory nut was turned and carved into sewing tools and was used to make thimbles and thimble cases, the latter mostly in the shape of an acorn. The colour varies from light cream to brown. Invariably the thimble case is made in two halves which screw together and the thimble rests inside. The plainer cases may have a simple design worked on the cup part of the acorn, leaving the body itself perfectly smooth. Others are more elaborately worked and carved all over. Some vegetable ivory thimble cases carry a bone or ivory fitting at the top with a peep-hole view of a fashionable holiday or tourist resort of the period and among those noted are Burnham, Harwich, Richmond, Stirling, Torquay and Yarmouth. Vegetable ivory cases may also be found in the shape of an egg but these are merely polished without any carving, thus tending to be somewhat plain and unattractive. Attempts were made to use colour on vegetable ivory thimble cases but this was not successful and more often than not all that is left is the vestige of a design. Vegetable ivory was used chiefly during the Victorian era and a thimble case inscribed 'A present from the Thames Tunnel' suggests that thimble cases made from vegetable ivory were being sold about 1846. By about 1870 the demand for objects made of vegetable ivory grew to the point that prices became inflated and by the end of the century vegetable ivory had given way to celluloid and other plastic materials.

Another popular subject for thimble cases in Victorian times was the slipper or shoe. The more common model was made of pressed glass about two inches long and usually in white, green, blue or dark amber. The glass might be hand-painted or otherwise decorated and

107 Pressed glass thimble
holder in the shape of a shoe.
(Private collection)

the thimble fitted into a special cavity approximately where the foot
would fit in a shoe. Another model somewhat similar in both shape
and size, but more elaborate, was made with a base of pewter or similar
metal covered with leather or fabric and fitted with a leather sole. Still
more elaborate were small-scale but otherwise accurate models of shoes
and slippers made up in a variety of fashions and materials. These might
include an inner sole made of flannelette which served as a needle
holder. The Fairy Slipper (Rd. No. 28040) was designed to hang against
a wall and hold a silver thimble.

Also typical of the late Victorian period is a range of small thimble cases made of yellow metal sheeting in the shape of an egg or

108 Metal thimble case in the
shape of an egg.
(Private collection)

109 Thimble case made of
brass with glass top. French,
late nineteenth-century.
(Private collection)

of a small rectangular box fitted to be held by a small chain. The sheeting which was impressed with a light design was moulded to shape
and held in a brass framework. The inside fittings to hold the thimble
were made of cardboard and other similar materials in bright colours.
These cases which were available as cheap souvenirs were designed to
hold a brass thimble and were sold, it is believed, from about 1890
to 1910. A specimen made to commemorate the Diamond Jubilee (1897)
carries a small picture of Queen Victoria and another has a small medal
commemorating the Franco-British Exhibition held in London in 1908.
Cases which have lost their inside fittings or their chains are best
avoided. Somewhat similar cases with the same framework and the
same internal fittings, but with the yellow metal sheeting replaced by
half shells of mother-of-pearl, can also be found and date from approximately the same period.

Thimble cases have frequently been made in the shape of an
egg or an acorn but there have been many other models. It would
be fascinating to know, for instance, why so many thimble cases were
made in the shape of an egg cup with an egg resting inside. Such
thimble cases are made of wood, usually ebony, turned in the shape

110 Thimble case in the
shape of an egg-cup.
(Private collection)

111 Wooden thimble and
thimble case in the shape of
an acorn.
(Private collection)

of an egg cup and with a polished vegetable ivory egg fitted on top. The egg part unscrews and the thimble is found on a velvet covered mount in the egg cup itself. Other thimble cases have been made in the shape of a barrel: there are ivory barrels and barrels made of bone and some made of ebony covered with leather. Small leather caskets with brass fittings or similar caskets in purple or mauve velvet were also popular and there are plush covered boxes in various shapes such as for instance 'The Cupid Heart Case', (Rd. No. 210332) which was designed to hold a silver thimble. Then again thimble cases have been made in the shape of baskets, bottles, horseshoes, electric bulbs, books, owls, sailing boats, lanterns and miniature hampers. The list is seemingly inexhaustible and one can only wonder at the exuberance of Victorian taste and imagination.

Finally, this account would not be complete without some reference to the type of casket which a jeweller would normally have provided, assuming that his customer was not looking for anything fancy in which to present a thimble. Traditionally the more expensive thimbles such as those made of gold were sold in a plain leather case shaped to fit round a thimble. This would normally be made of brown leather although red leather cases may sometimes be found. Slightly larger cases were made to hold porcelain thimbles. The thimble case for a gold thimble would normally have the name of the jeweller printed on a silk facing inside the lid. Small celluloid boxes of a similar shape were used for a time in plain cream or coloured celluloid and occasionally bearing some short inscription. Because leather cases were expensive, already by the 1890s silver thimbles were sold in small individual cardboard boxes which might or might not be decorated with a gold edging.

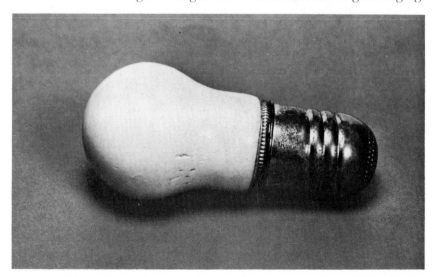

112 Needle and thread holder in the shape of an electric light bulb. (*Private collection*)

134

By the time of the first World War this practice was widespread. At first these little boxes bore the name of the jeweller selling the thimble, but by the 1930s most thimbles were sold in boxes supplied by the manufacturers, often under a brand name. These in turn disappeared and it is perhaps appropriate to conclude this chapter on thimble cases by noting that more often than not the present-day thimble is sold loose without thimble case or any other form of packaging, except possibly a scrap of tissue paper or a small plastic envelope.

113 Ebony thimble holder in the shape of an owl.
(*Private collection*)

114 Thimble-stand in the form of a sailing-ship. Mother-of-pearl inscribed 'A present from Eastbourne'. Height 8·7 cm.
(*Private collection*)

Thimble-rigging

Among the more seamy activities associated with race courses was the sharpers' game of thimbling. This sleight-of-hand trick was played with three small thimble-shaped cups and a tiny ball or pea. The ball was placed on a table and covered with one of the cups. The trickster then started moving the ball about and challenged bystanders to guess which cup covered the ball and to bet on their choice. Needless to say, the person who bet was seldom allowed to win. The game was known in England at the time of Queen Anne and may conceivably have been imported by continental gypsies during the reign of Queen Elizabeth I. Gay mentions it in his *Trivia* (1716) and Dickens, writing of Hampton race-course, refers to 'a little knot (of bystanders) gathered round a pea and thimble table to watch the plucking of some unhappy greenhorn'.[37] More recently the game of thimbling has fallen into disuse and it has been replaced by the equally unsavoury game known as hunt-the-lady. But the name has stuck and over the years the term thimble-rigging has come to be used allusively about any kind of mean cheating or jiggery-pokery. It is not inappropriate therefore to note that the vogue for thimble collecting and the relatively high prices which unusual thimbles will fetch have attracted the attention of the unscrupulous, nor is it inappropriate to warn against the activities of individuals and firms who have set out to cash in on the demand for thimbles and to prey on unwary collectors.

It would be hard to include under the heading of thimble-rigging those thimbles which are manufactured for the tourist trade. Most American collectors know the ornate silver thimbles sold to tourists in Mexico and even if housewives in Mexico may prefer plainer and more utilitarian thimbles, it is difficult to object to an item which is in some ways reminiscent of the 'special issues' which plague stamp collectors. Other countries which go in for tourist thimbles include West Germany, Holland, Greece and Spain. Presumably there are sufficient thimble collectors travelling around the world to make it worthwhile for duty free gift shops at international airports such as Athens, Barcelona, Madrid or Rotterdam to stock them. The Greek tourist thimbles are distinctive and as regards Spain, the yellow metal 'Toledo' thimbles will be equally well known. Provided they are sold for what they are, namely inexpensive souvenirs, they are perfectly harmless and they may even have some attraction for collectors wanting an assortment of modern thimbles. As such there can be no objection, but it is an altogether different story when it comes to plain fakes or worthless thimbles improved and passed off as rare or exotic items for sale at correspondingly high prices. Unfortunately by its very nature the an-

115 *The blood-letting,* by
Egbert van Heemskerk II (1645-1704).
(Stedelijk Museum, Amsterdam)

tiques trade harbours more than its fair share of sharks and tricksters and the budding collector needs to keep the doctrine of 'caveat emptor' well before him. The traditional advice of dealing only with experienced and reputable firms is of course perfectly sound, but it hardly meets the circumstances of the thimble collector who as a specialist may need to cast his net wider, even if it means exercising more caution. Some advice may therefore be helpful.

In the first place it is important to recognise that a thimble in mint condition is worth considerably more than a worn or damaged thimble. This is the same as for coin collecting where a worn coin, unless it is particularly rare, is almost worthless. Beware therefore of the silver or gold thimble with signs of wear or with holes in it. It is always good practice to hold a thimble to the light to see if it is holed. Beware also of the thimble which has been repaired. Always look carefully, preferably with a glass, for the tell-tale solder marks on the inside. Such a thimble may still be collectable but its value will be correspondingly lower and a dealer – unless he knows you – will not necessarily draw your attention to its condition.

Even more care should be exercised when buying enamel or porcelain thimbles. Such thimbles are expensive and nowhere is the art of the restorer more in evidence. Repairing chipped, cracked, broken or otherwise damaged porcelain has become an industry on its own account. At their best, restorers will repair a piece of porcelain and glaze over the cracks so that the repair is indistinguishable except under an ultra-violet lamp. At their worst they will merely touch up or hide damage with suitably coloured paint. Restorers will also repair chipped or damaged enamel. In any event it is the buyer's responsibility to satisfy himself regarding the quality and condition of what he is buying. Bear in mind that whilst dealers may not choose to draw your attention to a flaw, a reputable dealer will never tell a deliberate untruth. Always ask whether a porcelain or enamel thimble has been repaired and listen carefully to the reply. Look at the thimble against a strong light when hidden cracks may become apparent. Study the surface carefully for any disturbance in the design. Above all take your time. It is only after the most careful examination that you can decide whether the porcelain thimble you are offered is cheap at 100 dollars or expensive at 25. With experience the pitfalls will become more obvious but even the expert can be taken in from time to time.

The art of the restorer is not necessarily put to dishonest uses and is therefore in a different category to outright fakes and forgeries. A plain silver thimble may be worth five dollars but a silver thimble set with turquoise is worth twenty-five dollars or more. All that are required therefore are some old beads together with a good quality adhesive to transform an ordinary thimble into something which is seemingly more valuable. Such fakes are crude and can normally be distinguished under a glass as there is usually a small amount of adhesive to be seen round the stones. They are also often given away by the pattern of the silver thimble which does not fit. But if the pattern is right and the thimble is presented cleverly in a thimble case it may be dangerous. At least one individual has been faking thimbles in and around London in recent years and dealers themselves are sometimes taken in. If a friendly dealer tells you that he is selling a thimble on behalf of someone else take note. He may be telling you without putting it in so many words that he does not guarantee the authenticity of the thimble. You may not catch on but this could be the dealer's way of warning you that you are on your own.

Established collectors will know what to look for and the above is mainly directed at newcomers to the gentle game of thimble hunting. Doubtless there will be those who regard this as a routine warning; others may be interested to know more about the dangers; and there may also be dealers who think that the author is being unfair to their profession. The following therefore is an extract from a casebook on thimble-rigging covering a period of only eighteen months:

Gold plated silver thimble size 9 offered as 9 carat gold thimble.

Late nineteenth-century silver thimble with turquoise beading cemented round (about half a dozen).

Ditto in case to achieve more realism.

Sundry silver thimbles gold plated and offered as gold thimbles. (Sometimes given away by silver hallmarks.)

Late nineteenth-century silver thimble with imitation garnet beading cemented round (three).

Vegetable ivory thimble drilled around with alternate turquoise and coloured glass beading inserted in holes.

Gold thimble with imitation garnet beading cemented round.

Nineteenth-century ivory thimble with turquoise beading cemented round.

Twentieth-century silver thimbles with gold wedding rings soldered round base.

Nineteenth-century steel-tipped silver thimble, gold plated.

Silver thimble heavily gold plated with turquoise beading cemented round.

Small liqueur glass offered as 'thumb' thimble.

Modern gold thimble with seed pearl beading cemented round. (Offered at 60 dollars and a dangerous fake.)

Gold charm thimble off bracelet with retaining ring filed down and offered in enamelled case as child's thimble and thimble case.

Silver charm thimble off bracelet with retaining ring filed down (several).

Modern silver thimbles filed down and hand enamelled with designs of Windsor Castle, etc. (Not really fakes but spurious all the same.)

Contemporary porcelain thimbles with printed design filed off to appear old.

Silver thimble with gold shield but otherwise gold plated offered for sale as gold.

Small clear glass beaker offered as thimble.

Late nineteenth-century thimble with enamel added to fill pattern round the base.

Silver thimble, enamelled round base.

Damaged thimble with hole filled in with turquoise and another turquoise inserted on the other side for purposes of symmetry.

Heart-shaped turquoise inserted in silver thimble to imitate shield.

Silver thimble gilded and with turquoise beading cemented round.

Silver thimble with top cut off and stone inserted in the tip in imitation of stone-capped thimbles (three).

Silver thimble with pendant soldered on side.

Top of enamel needle case done up as thimble.

Silver thimble with turquoise stone set in tip. (An obvious fake since useless as thimble).

Various spurious items masquerading as enamel thimbles.

Plastic thimble sold as ivory.

Norwegian enamel thimble stripped of its enamel and passed off as rare French thimble.

Silver thimble with turquoise or semi-precious stones in fitments soldered round the sides (several).

Finally, not less than two dozen containers of various descriptions including inkwells adapted or otherwise passed off as 'thimble cases'.

But the most bare-faced case of thimble-rigging was in London at one of the antiques galleries frequented by tourists. It consisted of a Worcester porcelain thimble, hand-painted with a fine looking bullfinch, date about 1900, offered at 100 dollars or twice its proper value and around it three contemporary Worcester porcelain thimbles also hand-painted offered at 50 dollars or ten times their proper value. On enquiring about the more expensive thimble, it was, needless to say, already 'sold' thus confirming that its function was to act as a decoy for the sale of its worthless brethren.

And lest this example be thought exceptional, there was at one of the leading antiques fairs a nineteenth-century Derby porcelain thimble marked at 300 dollars in the same show case as a worthless modern porcelain thimble marked at 50 dollars – here again at least ten times its proper value. The organisers of reputable antiques fairs seek to prevent exhibitors from passing off modern wares as antiques and indeed normally exclude anything which is less than a given age, but it is evident that in the case of thimbles this does not necessarily afford sufficient protection.

It would be ungracious to end this chapter without paying due acknowledgment to the many dealers who are just as anxious as the collector to see fair play and who themselves are often the prey of the unscrupulous. The truth is that careless or dishonest dealers are in the minority, but it would be foolish to pretend that they do not exist and if this chapter can help to curtail their activities by publicising them, it will have served a useful purpose.

Collecting thimbles

A wise collector does not seek to rationalise his motives and should be content that collecting brings him pleasure and satisfaction. Nevertheless it is permissible to ask why thimble collecting has become so popular and the reasons are not far to find. Apart from the general attraction of smallness and quality in an age which glories in largeness and mass production, a special and additional fascination of thimbles is that they are one of the earliest domestic tools of mankind. There is an underlying sense of purpose and industry about thimbles which distinguishes them from mere trifles and up to a point the fact that the thimble is becoming obsolescent also adds to its significance in the eyes of collectors. Because the thimble is universal and because it was used by rich and poor alike throughout the centuries, it has become

116 *Sewing woman with children*, by Adriaen van Gaesbeeck (1621-1650). *(Staatliche Kunsthalle Museum, Karlsruhe)*

an integral part of our civilisation. Generations of craftsmen have devoted their skill to producing better, finer, more attractive thimbles, ranging from plain utilitarian objects to the heights of the jeweller's and goldsmith's art. Beautiful, precious objects have always been collected but thimbles have the added interest of their traditional place in the household.

Another factor which undoubtedly adds to the popularity of thimble collecting is the excitement of the chase. This applies to some extent to all forms of collecting, but the thimble being so small, distinctive and universal, it is ideal for the purpose – the same qualities perhaps which established hunt-the-thimble as a favourite game in the nursery. Today hunt-the-thimble is an adult pursuit followed by many collectors throughout the world. The United States is still the most thimble-conscious country: certainly it is the only one with a mail order business directed specially at thimble collectors but there are now collectors in most countries and the truth is that thimble hunting is so popular that good thimbles have all but disappeared. It is tempting to think of old ladies treasuring the thimbles which belonged to their grandmothers and no doubt there are more thimbles coming forward all the time. But in practice most of the better material has long been in the hands of collectors (there are remarkably few thimbles in the hands of museums), the trade in thimbles is well organised and any newcomer to thimble collecting should bear this in mind.

It is not the purpose here to discuss how to set about collecting thimbles nor to suggest the different types of thimbles in which a collector might specialise. The enormous variety makes it difficult at first

117 Silver thimbles from South America. Left to right: plain design, Brazil, modern; decorated with two bands of gold and inscribed A.B., Argentine, nineteenth-century; decorated with gold-plated llama, Argentine, modern; plain design, unknown origin, modern; plain design, unknown origin, modern; decorated with two bands of gold, Chile, nineteenth-century.
(Private collection)

to know which thimbles to collect and where and how to start. A good beginning is to look at thimbles in museums and private collections and to become aware of thimbles. The first criterion must be to collect what you like. Neither is it intended to consider the question of price because prices can vary enormously. There is, however, one rule about buying thimbles which is worth remembering; keep to thimbles in good condition and concentrate on beauty and quality. Then after buying a thimble, bring it home, clean it, study it and gloat over it to your heart's content; if it continues to give you pleasure and if you can regard the price you paid for it with equanimity, you can be sure it was a good buy. If on the other hand your pleasure diminishes, if you start thinking that the price you paid may have been excessive, it was probably a bad buy. There is no market price for thimbles. It is easy to get carried away in the excitement of the chase and each collector must set his own limits. Above all disregard talk about thimbles being a good investment. This is the kind of nonsense which is put about by journalists who are short of copy or by dealers who are trying to persuade you to pay more than you can afford. The wise collector should forget about market trends and concentrate on buying carefully and sensibly within his means.

Having started a thimble collection, the collector will be faced with the choice of where to house it. Some collectors keep their thimbles in specially designed display cabinets, others in boxes, drawers or jars, and yet others find it preferable to keep their thimbles in a safe deposit. This is really a matter for the individual. Thimbles being so small they seldom present a problem. Furthermore thimbles are very easy to look after and require little attention. New additions should be carefully examined and cleaned when first acquired. Some types of thimbles are best left undisturbed – cleaning an old brass thimble will merely destroy the patina – but most silver thimbles need to be polished if they are to look their best. Cleaning silver thimbles can be tiresome because of the difficulty of reaching tarnished areas within the indentations, but once it is cleaned the thimble will remain in good condition and can be polished back again quickly when necessary.

Some collectors find that systematic record-keeping increases the enjoyment they get from their collection and they catalogue each new acquisition as it arrives. There is no set form for cataloguing thimbles but the following is a check list of the points to be covered:

Name of collection and/or reference number.
Composition of thimble (gold, silver, brass, etc.).
Origin (if known).
Condition (state if damaged).

Brief description of thimble.
Inscriptions and/or hallmarks (if any).
Country of manufacture (if known).
Name of manufacturer (if known).
Size number (modern thimbles only).
Date or attribution.
Height (in centimetres) and/or weight (in grams).
Cross-references (if any).

To the above it may be desirable to add the following:

Brief commentary on the thimble or its attribution.
Details of any photographs available.
How, when and where acquired.
Value for insurance purposes.

The following are two examples of catalogue references taken from international museums:

British Museum, Department of Mediaeval and Later Antiquities, 81, 11-4, 4. Silver. Two ovals containing a head: one obliterated other crowned and inscribed C.R.2. English, 17th century. Height 1·8 cms.

Kunstgewerbemuseum Berlin, Inv. No. L388: Thimble made of gold, decorated with a tendril of leaves. A cornelian inset in top, Height 2 cms. Inside four marks: Three Crowns (Sweden); a crowned G. (Gothenburg); Makers stamp IDB (Johann Daniel Blomsterwall, Master 181?-1841); and 18k (carat). Regarding the goldsmith: G. Upmark, Guld och Silversmeder i Sveridge, S.334, Meisterzeichen Nr. 2599.

Thimbles can be examined satisfactorily with the naked eye but a glass of the type used by watch repairers with a magnification of $\times 5$ or $\times 10$ will be found useful when looking at hallmarks. A simple millimetre gauge is also helpful in determining the height for cataloguing purposes. Otherwise there is no special equipment required for thimble collecting unless it is desired to keep a photographic record. The subject of photographing thimbles is beyond the scope of this book and it will be sufficient to say that for amateur purposes a 35 mm. single lens reflex camera with a built-in exposure metre of the type that measures the brightness on the focusing screen and with a set of extension tubes for close-up focusing will serve admirably. With such equipment it is possible to take photographs up to natural size and even larger either in black and white or in colour.

Finally if a collector is really interested in thimbles he will study the pieces in his collection, exchange views with other collectors and seek out information in archives, libraries and museums. Considerably more research is required and it is to be hoped that many more collectors will feel inspired to probe the records and help to rediscover the importance, splendour and exclusiveness which has attached to the thimble throughout its long history.

118 Gold thimbles. *(Private collection)*

Bibliography

D'Allemagne, H. R., *Les Accessoires du Costume et du Mobilier,* Paris 1928.

Andere, M., *Old Needlework Boxes and Tools,* Newton Abbot 1971.

Bond, S., *History of Sewing Tools,* Embroiderers' Guild, London 1967.

Groves, S., *The History of Needlework Tools and Accessories,* London 1969.

Lundquist, M., *The Book of a Thousand Thimbles,* Iowa 1970.

Syer Cuming, H., 'On Thimbles', *Journal of the British Archeological Association,* March 1879.

Whiting, G., *Tools and Toys of Stitchery,* New York 1928.

Notes

1 G. R. Davidson, *Corinth*, Vol. XII: *The Minor Objects*, Princetown 1952.

2 William C. Hayes, *The Scepter of Egypt*, Vol. II, 411-12, New York 1953.

3 *Leechdoms, wortcunning, and starcraft of Early England* (ed. Cockayne), Rolls series 1844.

4 Joan Liversidge, *Britain in the Roman Empire*, London 1968. Plate 72 illustrates a Roman thimble.

5 Thomas Hoccleve, *De Regimine Principium*, 1412.

6 *Le Livre des Métiers d'Etienne Boileau*, Titre 42.

7 Noël du Fail, *Propos Rustiques*, 1547 (chapter 6, p. 47).

8 Barnaby Rich, *My Ladies Looking Glasse*, London 1616.

9 H. R. d'Allemagne, *Les Accessoires du Costume et du Mobilier*, Plate CCVI.

10 G. Bernard Hughes, 'More about collecting antiques', *Country Life*, 1960.

11 *Revue des Sociétés Savantes*, Série 7, Tome VI, p. 234.

12 Joan Wake, *The Brudenells of Deene*, London 1953.

13 Peter Boyd-Bowman, 'Indice y Extractos del Archivo de Protocolo de Puebla', unpublished MS. Vol. II.

14 I. N. Hume, *A Guide to artifacts of Colonial America*, New York 1970.

15 Thomas May, *The History of the Parliament which began 1640*.

16 Stephen Daniell, *A History of Taxation and Taxes in England*.

17 Patent of John Lofting – Engine for making thimbles – Number 319.

18 John Houghton F. R. S., *A collection of letters for improvement of husbandry and trade*, revised edition (Richard Bradly), Vol. 2, London 1727/8, chapter CCLX.

19 Francis Colner, 'Memorials of Marlow' local newspaper articles, 1932/3.

20 Daniel Defoe, *Tour through England and Wales 1724-6*.

148

21   Tom Treddlehoyle (Charles Rodgers), *The Barinsla folk's annual,* 1847.

22   Joseph N. Gores, *Marine Salvage,* Newton Abbot, 1972.

23   A. W. Coysh and J. King, ed., *Buying Antiques Reference Book,* Newton Abbot, 1968.

24   S. Ducret, *Fürstenberger Porzellan,* Zurich 1965, Vol. II.

25   Friedrich H. Hofmann, *Geschichte der bayerischen Porzellan Manufaktur, Nymphenburg,* Vol. III, 593.

26   S. Ducret, *Züricher Porzellan,* Zurich 1944, p. 99.

27   B. L. Grandjean, *Kangelig Dansk Porcelain,* Copenhagen 1962.

28   L. Jewitt, F.S.A., *Ceramic Art in Great Britain,* Vol. I, London 1878.

29   Wm. Bemrose, *Bow Chelsea and Derby Porcelain,* London 1898.

30   *Documents per l'Historia de la Cultura Catelana Mig-eval,* Vol. I, published by Antoni Rubió y Lluch, Barcelona 1908, p. 208.

31   *Les poinçons de garantie internationaux pour l'argent,* 9th edition, Tardy: Paris; and Sir Charles James Jackson, *English Goldsmiths and their Marks,* London 1949.

32   Elizabeth Aldridge, 'Collecting Thimbles' *Journal of Antique Collecting,* No. 7, Vol. 8 (November 1973).

33   James Toller, 'French Prisoners-of-War Work', *Collector's Guide* (July 1971).

34   William Congreve, *The Way of the World,* Act III, Scene 3, London 1700.

35   Jane Austen, *Sense and Sensibility,* Vol. III, chapter 38.

36   William Falconer, *An universal dictionary of the marine,* London 1769.

37   Charles Dickens, *Nicholas Nickleby,* chapter 50, 1838.

Index

Page numbers in italics refer to illustrations.

Adderley (Royal) porcelain, 35
advertising, 96, 101, 102, 105, 115-17, *115*, *116*
agate, 84, *85*, *86*
Allemagne, H.R.d', 12, 146
aluminium, 86, 96, 101, 103, 115, 116, *116*, 117
amethyst, 84, *84*, *85*
Argentina, *142*
Austria, 71, 88, 89

Battersea enamel *see* Bilston enamel
Benschoten, Nicholas van, 18
Bilston enamel, 38, *38*, 41, *49*, *51*
Birmingham, *58*, 59, 66, *69*, 72, *77*, 86, *86*, 118, 123
Blois, 22
bloodstone, 84
bog oak, 88, *88*
Bolsover, Thomas, 25
bone, 1, 6, 7, 80, *80*, 105
Borger, Pieter, 20
boxwood, 87, 88
brand names, 64, *98*, 99, 101-6 *passim*, 112, *113*
brass, 9, 13, *13*, 18-22, *51*, 90-96, *106*, *107* et al.
Brazil, *142*
Britannia metal, 26
British Archeological Association, 3, 24, 82, 146
British Museum, 7, 15, *15*, *27*, *62*, 83, 109, 144
Brogan, Thomas S., 71
bronze, 1, 2, 6, 7, *27*, *51*, 90
Byzantium, 1, 6

calamine *see* zinc
casein, 80, 105
celluloid, 80, 105, 119
Central Museum, Utrecht, *63*
chatelaines, *25*, *28*, *40*, *52*, *121*, 122, 123
Chelsea porcelain, 32
children's thimbles, 6, *88*, 108, *108*, 139
Chile, *142*
China, *29*, 53, *54*, 55, 84, 106, *107*
clan tartan ware, 124, *124*, 125
Coalport porcelain, 32, 35
Colonial Williamsburg Foundation, *29*, *67*, 83
Copenhagen porcelain, 31, 32
copper, 96, 99, 103
coral, 46, 108, *108*
Corinth, 1, 7
cornelian, *29*, 42, *46*, 48, *77*, 84, 85, *85*, *87*, 88, *111*, 144
Corozo nut *see* vegetable ivory
cupro-nickel, 76, 94, 101, 102, *102*, 110

Dame's thimel, 24, 97
Davidson, G.R., 1
Delaporte Frères, 24
Derby Museum, 35
Derby porcelian, *29*, 32, 33, *34*, 35, *51*
diamonds, 45
dolls' thimbles, 108, *108*
domed thimbles, 7, 22, 106, 107
Doulton porcelain, 32, 33, 35
Dresden porcelain, 37
Duca di Martina Museum, 32

earthenware, *36*, 37
ebony, 87, 88, *88*
Ecuador, 55, 113
Egypt, *78*
electro-plating, 101, 112, 120
enamel, *28*, *29*, 38-43, *41*, *42*, *46*, *62*, *69*, *77*, *78*, 112, 122, 137, 139, *see also* Bilston enamel

Fabergé, Peter Carl, 41
fabric, 89, *89*
Field Museum of Natural History, Chicago, 96
Figdor, Albert, Collection, 12, *28*
filigree, *23*, *29*, *40*, 64, *65*, 66, *68*
finger guards, *55*, 81, 118-19, *118*, *119*
fingerling, 5, 8, 82, 90, 106
Fisher, Conan, 88
Fontaine, J. de La, 74, *74*
France, 6, 9, *23*, *28*, 30, *43*, 47, 48, *72*, *72*, 74, *74*, 114, *131* et al.
Fries Museum, Leeuwarden, *19*
Furstenberg porcelain, 31

Gabler, Gebrüder, GmbH, 55, *56*
Gallo-Roman thimbles, 6, *6*, *27*, 53, 80
garnet, 138
German silver *see* nickel silver
Germany, *11*, 13, 18, 30-31, 42, *49*, 59, *60*, *67*, 72, *85*, 87, 111-12, 117, 126 et al.
glass, *29*, 83, *83*, 139
gold, 10, 14, *23*, *28*, 44-7, *43-6*, *51*, *52*, 103, *108*, 118, *127*, 138-9, *145* et al.
Great Exhibition (1851), *27*, 93, 101, 110
Greece, 6, 79, 113, 135
Griffith, Henry, and Sons, *58*, 59, *63*, 64, 111, 112
Guildhall Museum, London, *13*
Gunner, A.T., Manufacturing Co., 71

hallmarks, 27-9, 47, 62, *69*, 71-4, 75, *109*, 118, 144
Halsted, Benjamin, 25
Halwylska Palatzet Museum, 85
Hammersley, 37
Herculaneum, 6, 106
Herend porcelain, 35
Hoeroldt, Johann Gregorius, 30, 31
Holland, 16, *16*, 18, *19*, 20, 42, 73, *79*, 135

horn, 56, 81, *81*
Horner, Charles, 99
Houghton, John F.R.S., 20
Howell, Dorothy, Collection, 14, *39*, *51*
Howell, James, 16
Hughes, G.B., 14
Hume, Ivor Noel, 15
Hungary, 35, 71, 89
Hurd, Jacob, 44, *44*

Iles, Charles, 93, 94, 99, 102, 105
India, 26, *29*, *40*, 53, 76, *77*, 81, *81*, 88
inscriptions *see* mottoes
international trade, 18, 42, 43, 59, 79, 111, 112
inventories, 10, 14, 15, 22, 32, 92
Iran *see* Persia
Ireland, 8, 85-6, 88, *88*
iron, 9, 56, 97-101 *passim*, *106*, 107
Islington, 20, 92
Italy, 4, *27*, *46*, 72, 79, *84*, 97, *97*, 107
ivory, 6, 7, *29*, 48, 53-5, *55*, *62*, 80, 105, *108*, 118, 138, 139

jade, 84
Japan, 82, 89, *104*, 105, *107*

Ketcham and McDougall, 70
Kohls, Mildred, 37
Korea, 82, *89*
Kunstgewerbemuseum, Berlin, 46, 85, 120, 144

Lapland, 80, *80*, 107
latten, *6*, 9-10, *13*, *27*, 57, 90-92 *passim*
leather, 1-8, *8*, 10, 56, 82, *82*, 105, 106
leather worker's palm, 4, 107
letter seals, *40*, *63*, *65*, 66, 67, 119, 122
Limoges porcelain, 37
Loftinck, Reynier, 20
Lofting, John, 18, 20, 21, 22, 92
London Museum, 9, 15, *15*, 59, 92, 109

magnet, 94, 101
makers' marks, 29, 66, *69*, 70-71, 75, 91, 118, 123
Meissen porcelain, 30, 31, 36, *49*, *51*, 76
Mennecy porcelain, 30, 31
Metropolitan Museum of Art, New York, 1, *11*
Mexico, 79, 113, 135
Milan, 10
Minton porcelain, 32, 33
Mongolia, 8, *8*, 82
moonstone, 41, 42, *42*, 85, *85*
Morrall, Abel, 99, 102, *106*
moss agate, 84, *85*
mother-of-pearl, *28*, *29*, 48, *48*, 99
mottoes, 10, 22, 36, 59, 96, 114
mulberry wood, 87

Musée des Antiquités, Rouen, 6, *6*
Musée des Antiquités Nationales, Saint Germain-en-Laye, 6
Musée de Sèvres, Paris, 31
Musée Le Secq des Tournelles, 97, *97*
Musée National de Céramique, Paris, 30
Museum für Kunst und Gewerbe, Hamburg, 31, *49*
Museum of Decorative Art, Copenhagen, 32
Museum of Fine Arts, Boston, 44, *44*

Naples porcelain, 32
needles, 1-5, 7, 8, 53, 90, 106
needle cases, 38, 66, *67*
needle pushers, 1
needle threaders, 93, *93*, 94, 102, 116, *116*
needlework boxes, 48, 53, 55, 118
nickel-silver, 101-3, 112
niello, 78, *78*, *111*, 113, 114
North American Indians, 14, 96
Norway, 41, 42, *42*, 73, 85, 139
novelties, 24, *40*, 65-8 *passim*, 118, 119
nuns' thimbles, 88, *88*
Nymphenburg porcelain, 31

onyx, 84
orangewood, 88
Ovcinnikov, enameller, 41, *62*

Palais Royal, 48, 122
Paris, old, porcelain, 31
patents, 18, 20, *29*, 56, *56*, *58*, 75, *75*, 76, 93, *93*, 94, 102, 105
pearl, 46, *46*, 108, *108*, 139
peep-show thimbles *see* Pursall, William
Persia (Iran), 38, 43, 76, 78, *78*, 103
petit point, 89
pewter, 99, 103, 120, *121*
photography, 144-5
Piercy, John, *29*, 56, *56*
pinchbeck, 25, 103
plastics, 76, 80, 88, 96, 104-7 *passim*, 115, *116*, 117, 139
Poldi Museum, Milan, 42
porcelain, *28*, 30-37, 49, *49*, *50*, *51*, 53, *61*, 133, 137, 139
Portugal, 69, 79, *108*, 114, *114*
Powell, William, *34*, 35
Prince's metal, 24, 25, 103
Pursall, William, *93*, 94

Regemorter, Babtista van, 18
registered designs, *65*, 75-7 *passim*, *93*, 102, *109*, 130, 133
Revere, Paul, 44, *44*
ring and chain attachments, 76, *77*, *78*
ring-type thimbles *see* tailors' thimbles
Rockingham porcelain, 32
Roman thimbles, 3, 6, *6*, 7, *51*, 53, 106
rubies, 10, 14, *28*, *51*
Russia, 41, *41*, *62*, 73, 76, *77*, 78, *78*, 111, *111*, 113

sailors' palms, thimbles, 3, 4, 24, 107
sandalwood, 88
sapphires, 14, *51*
scent bottles, *40*, *65*, 66
Schreiber Collection, 32, 41
Schweiz. Landesmuseum, Zurich, 66, *68*
Scottish thimbles, 85
seals *see* letter seals
Sears Roebuck, 45, 103
Sèvres porcelain, 30
sewing boxes *see* needlework boxes
sewing kits, *67*, *68*, 99, *100*, 101, 115, *115*
Seyne, Jacob, 18
Sheffield plate, 25, 26
Shipman, Charles, 53
silver, *11*, *12*, *15*, *19*, *23*, *26*, *40*, 57-59, *84*, *85*, *86*, *109*, *111*, *118*, *119*, *142 et al.*
silver gilt, *28*, 46, 47, *74*, *77*, *84*, *110*, 118
Simons Brothers & Co., 45, 59, 71
simulated stone tops, 42, 86, 112, 116
size numbers, 28, 29, 70, 71, *91*, 105, 144
souvenir thimbles, 36, 55, 88, 96, 102, 109-114, 135
· Spain, 75, 96, *100*, 113, *114*, 135
spindles, 2, 10
spirit measures, 120, *121*
Spode/Copeland, 32, *51*
steel, 56, 59, 97-103 *passim*
steel cores, 64, *98*, 99, 103
steel top thimbles, 24, 25, 64, *68*, *80*, *98*, 99, *108*, 138
Stevenson & Hancock, 35
stickware *see* Tunbridge ware
Stoke-on-Trent Museum, 37
stone, 1, 84-6
sugar-loaf *see* domed thimbles
Sweden, 4, *46*, 73
Syria, 6

tagua *see* vegetable ivory
tailors' thimbles, 1, *6*, 7, *8*, 20, *27*, 81, 82, 88, *102-7 passim*
tape measures, *40*, *65*, 66
Taylor, Joseph, 66, 118
Taylor's non-slip, 93, *93*
thimble bells, 96
thimble cases, holders, *23*, 37, *40*, *52*, *54*, 88, 122-34 *et al.*
thimble-rigging, 47, 102-3, 135-40
thimble shapes, *36*, 37, *121*
thimble stands, 37, *40*, 126
thread cutters, 93, 94
thumb thimbles, 3, 4, 9, 24, 90, 139
Toledo, 96, 113, 135
tortoise-shell, *29*, *51*, 56, *56*, 119, *119*
toys *see* novelties
transfer ware, 114, 124, 125, *125*
Tunbridge ware, 87, *87*, 123, *123*
Turkestan, 76, *77*
turquoise, 46, *62*, 137, 138, 139
turtle-shell *see* tortoise-shell

Unite, George, *69*, 123
United States, 28, 44, *44*, *69*, 70-75 *passim*, 92-3, 96, *100*, 116-17 *et al.*

vegetable ivory, *29*, 55, 80, *128*, 129, 138
ventilated thimbles, 93, 94, 102
Victoria and Albert Museum, 32, 41, *49*, 66
Vienna porcelain, 31
vulcanite, 105

Walker, James, 115
wood, 84, *87-8*, 123, *132*
Worcester porcelain, *29*, 32, 33, *33*, *34*, 35, 36, 140

Yale University Art Gallery, 44, *44*

Zeeuws Museum, Middelburg, *12*
zinc, 9, 22, 90
Zurich porcelain, 31